BMW

Nigel Fryatt

First published in the United States of America in 1990 by the Mallard Press
Mallard Press and its accompanying design and logo are trademarks of
BDD Promotional Book Company, Inc.

ISBN 0-792-45331-X

Printed in Italy

Page 1: After relying on outside specialists to build its convertible models, BMW changed tack in 1986 to produce the 325i convertible in-house. The elaborate roof mechanism folds the roof down behind the rear seats.

Pages 2-3: The BMW Z1 roadster caused a sensation when first displayed as a design exercise. It caused an even greater one when BMW announced it was to produce the car.

This page: BMW has always had a policy of producing open-topped versions of its models. This is a 326 Cabriolet of the late 1930s with coachwork produced for BMW by Autentrieth.

Contents

The BMW Route to Success   6
BMW's Classic Cars   18
M Sport: Mouth-watering   56
Alpina: BMW's Alter Ego   74
Motorsport: A Race Apart   82
Tomorrow's BMWs   100
Index   111
Acknowledgments   112

The BMW Route to Success

It's quite a story. This German manufacturer now produces some of the world's finest cars. It is a company with an impressive reputation for design, innovation, production quality and driving pleasure. But it could have been so different. BMW owes its very existence to a British-designed motor car and a strange little Italian bubble car that now appears as dated as Beatle haircuts and platform shoes. In both cases, however, they were necessary business moves that gave BMW enough breathing space to steer away from bankruptcy. But it was close — on more than one occasion.

BMW is actually an abbreviation of Bayerische Motoren Werke and if you think that's a mouthful then take a deep breath because it was actually set up on 21 July 1917 as a merger between Rapp Motorenwerke and Gustav Otto Flugmaschinenfabrik. Gustav Otto was the son of Nikolaus August Otto, known as the inventor of the four-stroke internal combustion engine and one of the pioneers of aviation. It is logical that Gustav should have been involved in aircraft engines and he founded his aircraft factory on the outskirts of Munich in 1913. (Indeed, BMW's aviation heritage carries on today because the famous blue and white emblem that is known throughout the world as the badge of BMW, is actually a stylised, rotating propeller.) Karl Rapp had begun building marine and aviation engines in a few wooden shacks close to Gustav Otto. The 1917 merger between the two produced Bayerische Flugzeugwerke building military aircraft that were powered by Rapp engines. After World War I, however, the manufacture of military aircraft was forbidden in Germany, and both Rapp and Otto left the company that they had formed, now with its name changed to Bayerische Motoren Werke. The running of the company passed into the hands of three men; Franz Josef Popp, an Austrian engineer, Max Friz, BMW's senior designer and Camillo Castiglioni an Italian from Vienna who made up for what he didn't know about engines with what he did know about money. It is said that at the peak of Castiglioni's career, the financial genius owned some 170 companies, and he certainly demonstrated his talents by raising capital for BMW.

Obviously, in the aftermath of the First World War there was a demand for road transport. Indeed, the Treaty of Versailles limited the production of aircraft engines in Germany. There were a few exceptions to the Treaty and

BMW made the most of these, capturing a number of aviation world records. But with the future in mind, the newly financed German manufacturer turned its attention toward building a motorcycle called the BFW Helios. It was a 500cc device, with the now famous flat twin horizontally-opposed cylinder configuration, and was designed by Max Friz of BMW. Friz had worked on the Daimler Grand Prix engine at the end of the war. BMW's sporting tradition can, therefore, justifiably be traced back to its first motor cycle engine. Friz did much to improve the Helios and the new machine, called the BMW R32 had a basic engine layout that is still used in most BMW bikes today; a flat twin engine and universal drive shaft in a tubular frame.

What happened next seems hard to credit; BMW entered into an agreement with today's arch rivals Mercedes-Benz! BMW was to build motorcycles and aircraft engines with Mercedes able to concentrate on cars. It was also agreed that BMW should look into the production of a new small car. To

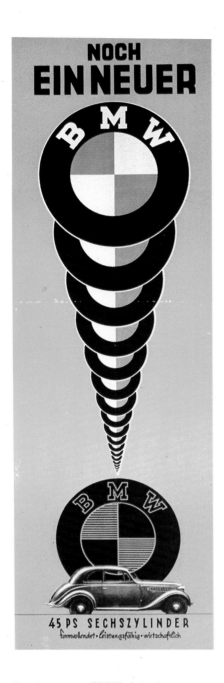

NOCH
EIN NEUER

45 PS SECHSZYLINDER
formvollendet · Leistungsfähig · wirtschaftlich

Dezember 1924   MOTOR   Seite 57

6|24 PS.

DIXI

Deutsche
Edelarbeit!

Dixi-Werke
EISENACH.

Previous page: BMW's latest sensation is the 850i, announced at the 1989 Frankfurt Motor Show.

Above left: BMW's first motorcycle was highly innovative. The 1923 R32 had a horizontally opposed, four-stroke, flat twin fitted transversely but instead of being chain driven it used a drive shaft to a bevel gear final drive in the rear wheel.

Left: BMW's aircraft heritage is reflected in the company's badging, the blue and white emblem being a stylised propeller, an emblem that the company has kept since the start.

Right: A stylish poster of the BMW Dixi, the car that started it all.

Above: An elegant BMW launch announcement.

this end, Popp went to the US and saw how it was being done there with Henry Ford and the famous Model T – one car finished every four minutes, and remember, this was 1928. BMW then found that there was a small company in business in Germany producing exactly the sort of car that Popp was looking for. The Eisenach Car Factory was building a small family car called the Dixi. This particular vehicle was not its own product but was a license version of the successful British Austin Seven. The Austin Seven remains today one of the most significant models in the history of the motor car with a reputation in Europe, akin to that of the Model T in the USA, as one of the first truly popular and affordable cars. For BMW, therefore, the Dixi can be seen

as a very good place to start to produce automobiles. Setting an example for a more recent entrepreneur, BMW liked the product so much that they bought the company. The Dixi was an immediate success and despite the very poor economic conditions of the time, BMW sold 5390 units in 1928 and 6792 the following year.

BMW produced both a roadster and an open tourer. The open tourer model was capable of 55mph, with the sport version nudging 65mph. The company gained a lot of important publicity and prestige with its version of this model winning the team prize in the 1929 Alpine Trial and a year later a BMW Dixi won its class in the Monte Carlo Rally. The Dixi only had a 750cc

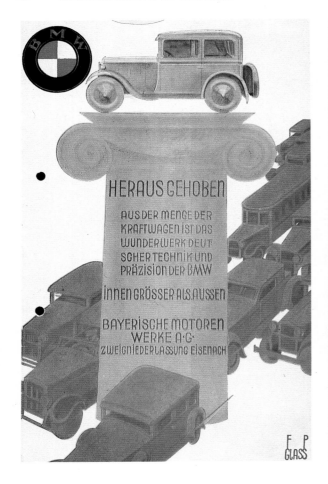

Left: A BMW poster celebrates the success of the Dixi in the Alpine Trial.

Far left: An advertisement for the first 'true' BMW, the 3/20 PS.

Right: Britain's love affair with the BMW began in the 1930s when the first models were imported from Germany under the Frazer Nash banner and many of them are still enthusiastically driven today. This is a 1935 Frazer Nash BMW 315 hillclimbing in England.

engine and produced a seemingly meager 15-18bhp but a top speed of over 60mph was impressive at the time. It must be remembered that competition success was an excellent method of demonstrating a production car's reliability and durability rather than just a means of emphasising a company's 'sporting' pretensions in the style that we are more used to today. If anything success in motorsport was even more important commercially than it is today.

These little cars sold well for BMW and by 1932 when the licensing contract to build the cars was cancelled, an impressive 32,000 had gone to customers. This sort of success gave the company the confidence, and the lost license the necessity, to go for its own design and that first 'in house' model was the 3/20 PS. (The designation follows the trend at the time to name a car after the power output of the engine – the 3/20 PS, therefore, had a 20bhp engine). The engine was, understandably perhaps, a development of the push rod ohv engine of the Austin Seven. The model's tubular backbone chassis and independent suspension were definitely up to date but with swing axles at each end, the handling left something to be desired. The 3/20 was very much a stop gap model between the ending of the Austin Seven contract and the arrival of the next BMW. Indeed, it was only a year later, in 1933, that the company produced its first six cylinder car – an engine configuration that has done a great deal to make BMW's reputation and is still very important today.

BMW's move into building the six cylinder engine was very much caused by the increasing financial insecurity of the 1930s. People who might otherwise have bought grand limousines were forced to trade down to something more modest. However, they were still demanding performance and as much prestige as they could afford. The first six cylinder was the 303, built both as a limousine and soft top. A tubular ladder-frame chassis, independent front suspension and live back axle with semi-elliptic springs was a deceptively simple design. The 1173cc engine produced 30bhp and was a radical change from the heritage of the Austin Seven. It was the responsibility of Fritz Fielder, BMW's new chief engineer. Fielder had brought with him an impressive reputation having been responsible for the 6 liter V12 and 5 liter straight eight Horch engines. This was something of a boom time for BMW. The company had large orders from the expanding air force of Hitler's Germany to build aero engines and the car business was expected to present a good sporting image – while still making a profit, of course.

With this in mind, BMW enlarged the 303's engine to 1490cc and designed a new model, the 315. Now with twin carburetors and a four speed transmission it produced 34bhp and 40bhp in a sports version. Although not overly impressive in terms of sheer power, this engine/chassis combination

was, at only some 1500 pounds, a light car and therefore a good performer; the 315 roadster is generally regarded as BMW's first significant motor car. With a top speed of 75mph, a 315 roadster won the 1934 Alpine Trial and had a significant number of other competition successes and began a long run of sporting models.

Having established its entire beginnings from building a British car in Germany, it is an indication of how far BMW had come by the mid 1930s that the process was effectively reversed. In 1935 Fielder produced a new engine, still a six cylinder but this time a 1911cc, fitted with three Solex carburetors, and producing 55bhp. Fitted to what was still basically the 303 chassis, the new model, the 319, was exported to Britain. With excellent handling and lively performance they were available in Britain as Type 55 Frazer Nash BMWs and the sports two-seater version was guaranteed for 80mph, a speed that many easily exceeded.

This move into a major foreign market was obviously an important step for BMW and underlined the importance that they should always have a sporting version of each model. It was logical, therefore, when the 326 sedan was introduced that there should also be a sports model. This need was further emphasized by the great publicity that rivals Mercedes-Benz and Auto Union were getting from their successes in Grand Prix racing. The ingredients were so nearly there; the 315 tubular chassis was light and strong and there was the reliable 2 liter six cylinder engine. All that was needed was more power. Fielder designed a completely new light alloy cylinder head for the engine. Fitted with three downdraft Solex carburetors this unit produced 80bhp in standard form and rather more when tuned by BMW's fledgling competition department. But it wasn't just the power that impressed. The shape of the aluminum body was well received and remains attractive to this day. It rolled out to race at the Nurburgring on 14 June 1936 when Ernst Henne won the 328's first event against considerable opposition. At the time of this victory the first examples of the new BMW sports car were still waiting to be delivered to the dealers.

Frazer Nash in Britain was quick to recognize the significance of the new BMW 328 and, as the German company's best export market, the model was soon on sale in the UK where it too succeeded in a variety of competitions, with a variety of driving talent – Stirling Moss started his motorsport career behind this BMW steering wheel in British production trials competitions. It is said that the 328 won more than 2000 events. One of the most significant was the 1939 Le Mans 24 Hour Race when a 328 Coupe took victory in its class at a record average speed of 82.3mph. A year later 328 Roadsters were first, third, fifth and sixth at the Italian classic, the Mille Miglia. Only 462 BMW 328s were built between 1936 and 1940 and, of

The BMW 326 was built between 1936 and 1941 and came in a number of bodystyles. The four seater cabriolet body was built by Autenrieth in Darmstadt a company that had previously built open-topped models for the company. Cabriolet 326s were popular with special customised versions being produced by other German coachwork companies such as Baur, Drauz, Reutter and Wendler.

Left: The 326 had the 1971cc version of the six cylinder producing 50bhp.

those, some 150 remain today. Despite this low number it is still one of the most significant sports cars ever built.

BMW's position as a major motor manufacturer was obviously growing but the 328 model was something of a highpoint at this stage in the story. Only one more model, the 335, was introduced by the company before the outbreak of World War II. The 335 was fitted with a 90bhp 3.5 liter engine and was the largest BMW to have been built. During World War II BMW was largely concerned with aircraft engine production (including development work on jet engines which in fact began before the war). Unfortunately these aspects of the BMW story are outside the scope of this book. In the aftermath of World War II, however, for BMW, as with many companies in Germany, sheer survival took precedence over investing in any new designs. And for BMW, things could hardly have been worse. BMW's Eisenach and Berlin plants were in the Russian sector and were nationalised by the new East German government. To add insult to injury, BMW look-alikes were actually produced behind the Iron Curtain and called EMWs. The Munich factory, of course, was in West Germany but had originally only built motorcycles and it was not until 1951 that car production returned.

The first post-war BMW was the 501 which was nothing more than a re-styled 326, with the first examples still powered by the 1971cc engine. At this time the company could not decide whether the future for BMW was in mass production automobiles or in building desirable, prestigious models in limited numbers and therefore with higher price; the latter did, of course, put the company head-to-head with Mercedes-Benz. For probably the most financially traumatic period of its history, BMW tried to do both.

To meet the challenge of the 'up-market' models a new V8 engine was designed. This all alloy 2.6 liter power unit made its debut at the 1954 Geneva Motor Show where it was well received. The BMW 502 model that was fitted with the engine was not a particularly original shape but the car's 100bhp did mean it was good for 100mph.

Development on the V8 engine continued and the capacity was increased for the 3168cc, 140bhp, BMW 503. This coupe was launched at the same time as the Mercedes-Benz 300SL which was rather the stronger commercial proposition. Financially, things were extremely difficult towards the end of the 1950s and so it is ironic that the 503 and the 507 should have been produced at this time. The latter, a superb two seater, is now regarded as a

Above: It was obviously hard work building BMWs in the early days if this period poster is anything to go by!

Above left: BMWs at play, today. You can still see early BMW sports cars competing. This is a 1937 Frazer Nash BMW 319.

Left: With all the classic style of the age, the 335 had a 3.5 litre engine producing 90bhp. It was built for fast cruising on Germany's newly constructed autobahnen.

Right: The 326 was launched in 1936 and was a genuine sensation — at a price. Unfortunately sales success was limited because of its high price tag.

Left: Gone are the powerful images of bare chested men pouring molten metal into molds! BMW's advertising in the mid-1950s had a more mellow appeal. The illustration shows a BMW 503.

Left: Gone are the powerful images of bare chested men pouring molten metal into molds! BMW's advertising in the mid-1950s had a more mellow appeal. The illustration shows a BMW 503.

Right: This is a BMW? The deal to produce the three wheel Isetta 'bubble cars' may seem as though BMW had lost its corporate marbles but it made a great deal of financial sense. The three and four wheeled 'Motocoupes' as they were known kept the company financially afloat.

Below: One of the most striking BMWs ever produced, the glorious 507. Extravagant, expensive and with 150bhp from its V8 power unit, extremely quick.

classic of its time. Styled by the gloriously named Count Albrecht Goertz with advice from Max Hoffman, the USA importer of BMWs, the car had the performance to match the looks; the V8 engine, now offering 150bhp, giving the car 135mph potential. Exclusive (only 252 507s and 413 503 saloons were built) and expensive, neither the 507 nor the 503 was the answer to BMW's growing financial problems and by 1959 the company was on the verge of bankruptcy.

Such extreme financial problems – increased with the growing decline of the motorcycle market – only serve to highlight the decision that the mass production model that would save the company should be the Italian Isetta bubble car. Memories of the success of the numerous Austin Sevens built under license in the early days obviously led BMW to choose one of the oddest automobiles ever designed.

Many automotive historians disagree on whether BMW's period of Isetta bubble car production actually saved the company or nearly pushed it right over the edge. This author tends to the view that we should actually thank the bubble car for giving us the fabulous automobiles that are built today – without it, BMW could well have collapsed completely. Production of the Isetta was between 1955 and 1962 and although highly popular for a while with certain types of fashion-conscious customers, it is quite understandable that such an oddball machine should eventually become unfashionable at Munich.

The Italian connection did have a far more significant factor in its favor in that it led BMW to work with designer Michelotti and produce the 700. The car was actually the work of Michelotti and Denzel, BMW's Austrian importer in Vienna. This model was powered by a two cylinder 697cc rear engine and rear suspension from the Isetta but with a much more modern body. In styling it was not unlike the British Triumph Herald also designed by Michelotti and was available in sedan, coupe and cabriolet forms. The base model had only 30bhp but was capable of around 75mph. More importantly, over 180,000 were produced. The car allowed BMW to climb out of its financial grave. But it was a close run thing. In 1959 the management actually recommended the sale of the company – to the banks and to Mercedes! The climate at the time must have been tense. Nonetheless the increasing sales of the 700 managed to keep the company solvent.

1962 was a turning point for BMW; the last V8 was produced and the first of the all-important 1500 models rolled off the production line. The V8 was the stylish 3200CS, a 160bhp coupe with a top speed of well over 120mph. It looked, for the time being at least, that there would be no more expensive, exciting and prestigious sporting sedans. A total reorganisation and moder-

nisation of the BMW range started with the 1500 in 1962 and then the 1800 in 1963 and was the work of major shareholder Herbert Quandt. Built in the latest unitary construction methods this is the range of BMWs that secured the financial success of the company. The first models were the four-door versions and they were followed by the two-door with their 1602cc and 2002cc. It was the latter engine that re-established BMW's sporting reputation; the 2002Tii and 2002 Turbo were excellent small sports sedans justifiably detailed more fully elsewhere in this book.

The cars got bigger and the range more comprehensive as the successes through the late sixties allowed the company the scope to do so. In the 1970s, BMW made a very significant rationalisation of the range that has remained to this day: the 3 Series, introduced in 1970, included four and six cylinder models; the 5 Series, introduced in 1975, had the 1800-3500cc engined models; and the 7 Series, introduced in 1977, had the top of the range designs (from which the 6 Series coupes were developed).

And that is a good place to leave the history of BMW to introduce in more detail the models that have made the company a success. When considering what is on offer today, it is interesting to remember the beginnings; the aircraft, the Dixis and the bubble cars. As we will explain, there have been interesting modern developments. In conjunction with the Austrian affiliate company BMW-Steyr Motoren GmbH, BMW built a turbocharged diesel engine that was fitted to the famous Lincoln Continental in America. There's also the growing importance of the Motorsport department, the marvelous M Sport models, an engine that won the Formula One World Championship, a brand new V12 engine and a two seater sports car that re-invents the door!

BMW's Classic Cars

The Super Sedans

If the history of the company has been something of a financial roller-coaster, looked at in isolation, the model range has shown a rather more stable development. Certainly, there have been gaps in that range, gaps that match the difficult periods that BMW has experienced, but the climb to its present day heights is best reflected by the last model announced as this is being written, the superb BMW 850i coupe. This particular model firmly places BMW as *the* major sporting sedan car manufacturer in the world; producer of The Super Sedans. In this chapter we have selected 25 of the most significant models that have been built. The sporting philosophy of the company is reflected perfectly when you compare one of the earliest with the very latest; the 328 and the 850i, both of which show a high level of innovation, a pure sporting pedigree and classic body styles.

BMW Dixi *1928-1932*

The First Model

BMW's first ever car was an open four-seater and was the first model to come from the takeover of the Eisenach Car Factory. This company was one of Germany's most prestigious car companies at the time, Eisenach producing the small Austin Seven under a license agreement. The first model, the Dixi 3/15 had a side-valve 748cc engine producing 15bhp. It was a great sales success for BMW. The model was quickly improved a year later when the simple ladder-frame chassis and its live leaf-spring axle specification was enhanced when it gained a foot brake that acted on all four wheels. There was also now a proper sedan version with a hard leatherette-covered roof. There were many differing body styles after that, all with the same specification side-valve engine. A more powerful high compression version of the engine was produced in 1930. This was the BMW 3/15 Wartburg, a model that was a great success on the race track. When the license agreement with Austin expired, BMW produced the 3/20. Obviously it was designed from the experience the company had had with the Dixi – central box frame, leaf sprung – but with a much improved overhead camshaft engine of 788cc producing 20bhp and, from 1933, a four speed transmission.

BMW 303 *1933-1937*

The First Six Cylinder

The significance of the 303 model range was really under the hood as it had BMW's first six cylinder engine. This set the philosophy for many of the models that exist today. The first model had a 1182cc version of the engine giving some 30bhp. Fitted in a new tubular space frame chassis, the 303 was quite a surprise for many of BMW's major competitors. For instance, it was more than 400 pounds lighter than any comparable competitor while it had 50 percent more power than previous BMWs. The range was soon extended to include two larger models, a 34bhp, 1490cc and a 45bhp unit of 1911cc (the latter was a highly successful engine and went on to power many famous models). There was also a smaller four cylinder version in the range, the 309 with 845cc and 22bhp. Right from this early start, BMW had a cabriolet version with a fully retractable soft top. The coachwork of these all-steel bodies came from Ambi-Budd in Berlin. In fact, many of the roof and body parts were sourced from a variety of places throughout Germany. The BMW 303 was also the first car to have the 'kidney-shaped' front radiator grille. Originally this was purely a technical necessity but the shape has been refined and remains to this day instantly recognisable on all BMWs.

Previous page: Right from its international debut at the Nurburgring on the 14th June 1936, the BMW 328 was a sensation both for its looks and its performance. Those looks have only improved with time . . . as has the car's value. It is estimated that only 150 models remain today. This is a right hand drive Frazer Nash model made for the British market.

Left: The 303 was the first six cylinder BMW to feature a tubular chassis and it surprised the competition when it was launched in 1933.

Right: The car that started it all. Having been a successful manufacturer of aircraft engines since 1917, BMW took over the Eisenach Vehicle Factory in 1928. The company produced a version of the Austin Seven under license from the British manufacturer. This model had a number of versions, but it was the small Dixi that was the success in the German market and started BMW down the road of successful vehicle production.

The 328 was BMW's first real sports car. The lightweight body built on to a tubular chassis in combination with the six cylinder 2 liter engine led to outstanding power-to-weight ratio and correspondingly impressive performance. When the model came to Britain, it was badged as a Frazer Nash (left).

Bottom right: In 1940 a special 328 Coupe won the gruelling, and prestigious, 1000 mile Mille Miglia in Italy. The 328 Mille Miglia Roadster was capable of a top speed of 139mph. Highly impressive even now.

Overleaf: A beautiful 1938 BMW 328 seen with a contemporary Bücker Jungmeister biplane.

BMW 328 *1936-1940*

The First Sports Car

It is a fair indication of the quality of a car if it survives the passage of time, not just in styling and visual appeal but far more important, in its dynamic qualities. Such a vehicle is the 1936 BMW 328. It was produced at a time when BMW recognised the need for a model to promote the company in the field of international motorsport to compete against rivals Mercedes-Benz and Auto Union. The 328 had a delightful aluminum body on a tubular chassis. This was a very lightweight combination, and had an excellent power-to-weight ratio, being fitted, in standard form, with the six cylinder 2 liter engine designed by Fritz Fielder which gave 80bhp. As a standard road car it gave the owner a 95mph top speed. In motorsport, with special camshafts, pistons, carburetors and altered gear ratios, the BMW 328 would top 120mph. It is no surprise therefore that the car was a great competition success and popular in both Germany and the UK where it was imported by AFN and called the Frazer Nash BMW. British interest in the model was established after the RAC took one to the famous Brooklands racing circuit for some speed tests. The BMW 328 was recorded to have covered 102.226 miles in the hour with a fastest lap of 103.97mph. On the international sporting front, Von Hanstein took a 328 coupe to victory in the 1940 Mille Miglia Italian endurance classic. The estimated 150 models that remain from the production run of only 462 are understandably extremely valuable.

BMW 501/502 V8 *1952-1956/1955-1963*

Starting Again

The bulbous 501's major significance is that it was the first BMW to have been built after the end of World War II. It took BMW so long actually to design and build this model because the division of Germany meant the company's major car plants at Eisenach and Berlin were now in East Germany. The 501 was, therefore, built at Munich and introduced at the 1952 Frankfurt Motor Show. The car is really only a new body on the pre-war 326 mechanicals powered by the 1971cc six cylinder engine producing a rather inadequate 65bhp and having a four speed column shift transmission. It had a massive box-section and tubular chassis frame, with torsion bar independent front suspension and torsion bar springing to a live rear axle. This model was improved when BMW produced the world's first light-alloy V8 engine. These large engine versions of the 501 were introduced at a time when BMW still saw itself as a direct competitor to Mercedes-Benz. The V8 version had the gear shift on the floor and despite its bulk the car was capable of 100mph. The model was updated in 1955 with a larger (3168cc) V8 engine and designated the 502. The larger engine had a power output of 140bhp. The de luxe models had servo brakes and at the end of the production run some models had disk brakes at the front.

BMW 503 *1956-1959*

The Sporting Sedan Returns

As soon as car production was fully underway after the traumas of World War II, BMW introduced its sporting sedan, the 503 coupe. Launched at the 1955 Frankfurt Motor Show, the 503 was based on the 502's floor pan and also had the same 3.2 liter version of the V8 engine. The first versions had separate transmissions and steering column mounted gear shifts, but from 1957 the transmission was mounted with the engine and the shift moved to the more acceptable floor position. The styling had a gross opulence to it and a heavy American influence. In fact, the design came from a German-American, Count Albrecht Goertz (who also designed the 507) and while the 140bhp engine meant the car had a reasonable turn of speed (it was capable of 105mph), the heavy chassis meant that roadholding and handling were not up to the standard of other vehicles in its class – notably the Mercedes-Benz 300SL that was introduced at exactly the same time. Sales of the model did not meet expectations and the car suffered from the success of the Mercedes and the financial problems that were affecting BMW. In total, only 413 were ever built. One 505 version was built as an official model for German state visits on an extended chassis and while this was good for image, BMW needed sales figures.

Left: BMW's first post-war models were the 501/502 range. The austere styling matched the atmosphere of the times. The model was simply a new body on the pre-war 326 chassis.

Right and below: The coupe and cabriolet versions of the 503 were styled by Albrecht Graf Goertz in 1956. It was a heavy vehicle and the performance and handling did not match the sporting looks. The model's sales success was limited due to the success of BMW's arch enemy, Mercedes-Benz, and the 300SL launched at the same time.

BMW 507 *1956-1959*

A Stunning Rarity

This has to be one of the most stunning BMWs ever built. What a great pity that this marvelous machine should be produced at exactly the wrong time, because, while enthusiasts around the world will admire the 507, it will not be happily remembered by any retired German accountants who happened to be working at BMW at the time. Announced at the same Frankfurt Show as the 503, and mechanically similar, the two-seater body was a full 16 inches shorter – a fact that aided both looks and handling. Designed by Goertz with sales in America in mind, the 507 had an extremely high price. The price could be matched by acceleration with a high compression version of the 3.2 liter V8 engine, built by Alex von Falkenhausen, having a power output of 150bhp and a top speed of around 125mph. But it did not sell well enough. With the benefit of hindsight, this can be seen as the last of the top of the range BMW sports machines until the 1970s and the 3.0CSL. Financial problems meant that only 252 versions of this sports car were ever built. Great shame.

BMW 700 *1959-1965*

Getting Back to The Front

In 1959 it looked as if BMW was going broke and would have to be sold, indeed, that was the view of the company's management. The little Isetta bubble car built under license from the Italian company Iso was an attempt to accumulate sales for a popular car, but it was never going to be enough on its own to pull BMW out of the financial mire. The BMW 700 can be seen, therefore, as something of a stopgap which, if it did nothing else, managed to keep the creditors away. First announced as a coupe, the four seater machine used the flat-twin engine and suspension from the (Isetta) 600 in an entirely new chassis. The all-steel body was BMW's first monocoque, neat and simply styled by Michelotti with independent suspension all round. Although the model looked as though there was an engine under the hood, it was actually positioned behind the line of the rear wheels, which actually meant that no less than 63 percent of the car's weight was over the rear wheels. Despite this, the 700 series handled relatively well. The first two cylinder version had only 30bhp from its 697cc engine but this did improve with future models to the 700 Sport which gave 40bhp from its twin-carburetor version of the same engine. The little unit was surprisingly adaptable to tuning and the models achieved some notable class successes on the race track. There was even an open topped version built for BMW by Baur in Stuttgart. In excess of 180,000 were built before production stopped in 1965.

Right: Not perhaps the greatest looking machine that the company ever produced, the 700 was very much a stop gap vehicle built during a time of severe financial strain. The car had a flat-twin rear-mounted engine. It's major milestone, however, was that it was BMW's first monocoque design.

Below and below right: If the 700 is something of an ugly duckling, then the 507 has to be seen as an elegant swan. This fabulous looking machine was first seen in 1956, a real dream machine. It was a dream that turned into a nightmare, however, and only 252 examples were ever built.

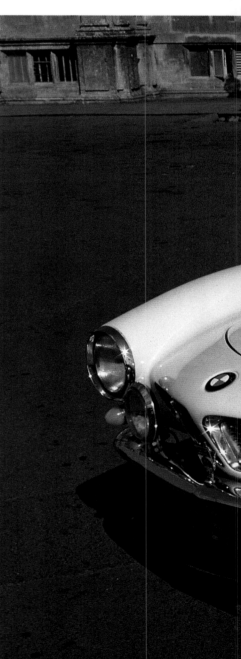

Left: The BMW 1500 can be seen as the model that brought the company into the modern, mass-production age. The German company went to Italy and Michelotti for the body design. A steel monocoque construction, MacPherson strut suspension and a lively four cylinder engine proved a winner and the 1500 was merely the start of a major model range.

Below left and right: Using existing components, BMW altered the four door body style of the 1500 to produce the two door model range of the 2002. This is the cabriolet version. First introduced in 1967, the open-topped BMW had to be modified in 1971 to include a comprehensive roll over bar in order to meet stringent safety regulations.

BMW 1500 *1962-72*

The New Range Starts

Despite the relative sales success of the 700 range, it was obvious that this model alone would not save BMW from being sold off. While the smaller shareholders were against any sale, there was hope and this allowed Herbert Quandt completely to reorganise the company and introduce an entirely new range. The reorganisation was auspicious. BMW found a niche in the market for small, but sporting sedans and in 1962 the breakthrough came with the BMW 1500. This model, like the 700 before it, was styled by Michelotti and had a four door unitary construction (steel monocoque) with a four cylinder, 1499cc overhead camshaft engine producing a lively 80bhp. MacPherson strut suspension was used at the front with the ingenious development at the rear of independent suspension with coil springs and semi trailing arms which pivoted from a cross beam mounted to the body sills. This set-up did lead to camber change but it was really the first time that independent rear suspension had been developed for a refined sedan car. Braking was through disks at the front, drums at the rear. This was an important model for BMW because, not only did it stop the rot and stop the company going broke, it was a model that had the facility to grow with larger engined versions following: an 83bhp 1573cc unit in 1964, soon followed by a 90bhp 1773cc unit that was capable of 100mph.

Developed from the 1800 model was the faster and more expensive Ti. At the time the 1800Ti was one of the fastest sedan cars in Europe, capable of matching competitors as formidable as the Lotus Cortina. The car was based on the 1800 with the engine having two twin-choke Solex carburetors which gave the car 110bhp at 5800rpm. But if this was thought to be an exciting development, it was really just the beginning.

BMW 2002 / 2002 Ti / 2002 Tii *1968-1975*

Quickening The Desire

Able to use existing components, BMW had produced its first two door model, the 1602 in 1966. Dropping the 2 liter engine into a lighter two door body to create the 2002 was a shrewd move; not only did it produce a vehicle that produced sufficient performance to tempt the younger executive set, it also produced a vehicle that could be taken to the race tracks of Europe to compete with the then victorious Alfa Romeos and Ford Escorts. This car re-established the motorsport reputation that BMW had not enjoyed since the dim and distant days of the 328 in the 1930s. The four cylinder 1990cc engine was to play an important part in a number of future BMW models. The engine had a single Solex carburetor and produced 100bhp which gave the car lively performance and a top speed around 107mph. The model was well received because, as well as being a good performer, it was also relatively economical. Front and rear anti-roll bars were also fitted for the first time. As more performance was needed for the race track, the production model was uprated to the twin Solex set up which had 120bhp on tap. A significant move was in 1971 when the model gained Kugelfischer fuel injection. Electronic fuel injection is taken for granted on many present day cars but in 1971 this mechanical system on the 2002 Tii was a big step forward. The power output was raised to 130bhp which increased the top speed to 116mph. The 2002 Tii also had wider wheels and larger front brakes to cope with the extra performance. Various body styles were produced; the Targa and the Touring (BMW do not recognise the terms estate car or station wagon). Unfortunately, the 2002 Tii, while a success for the sporting road car driver was no match for the 2 liter BDA engined Ford Escorts on the race track. Something had to be done.

BMW 2002 Turbo *1973-1974*

Blowing Like The Wind

The revitalised motorsporting ambitions of BMW led to the final development of the 2002 range – and by far the most exciting. In order to gain more power, a KKK turbocharger and Schafer fuel injection were mated to the four cylinder engine and helped make the road-going 2002 Turbo cause quite a sensation at the 1973 Frankfurt Motor Show. The engine offered the driver 170bhp from its 6.9:1 compression ratio power unit (the racing versions produced an impressive 270bhp). This was, therefore, a four seater sedan with shattering 130mph performance. It looked right as well with its wheel arch extensions (these allowed the racing cars to use wider wheels and tires), side stripes, bumperless front end and small trunk-lid spoiler. The car was, however, quite a handful for the inexperienced driver. Remember this was early days for a turbocharged engine and the car did have a significant turbo lag – the time gap between when the throttle is opened and the surge of extra power comes in. There was no smooth delivery of power, rather more a hesitation and then a massive surge. That's a characteristic the driver needs to be able to handle. The 2002 Turbo gained a reputation for being exciting, if somewhat hairy, especially in the wet. On the race track it proved its worth by winning the 1972 European Touring Car Championship only for a change in the rules to outlaw the car for the following year, which explains the car's short production run.

BMW 2500/2800/3.0/3.3 *1968-1977*

Return of the Big 'uns

As soon as the threat of imminent bankruptcy subsided BMW took an important step back into the production of large luxury sedans. And in doing that, the company went into direct competition with its arch rivals, Mercedes-Benz. The first in this distinguished range was the 2500, followed by the larger version of the six cylinder engine the 2800. Stylish and well-built, these quality sedans had four wheel servo disk brakes, limited slip differential, self-leveling rear suspension, power steering and automatic transmission as optional extras. They also had performance. The 2494cc six had 150bhp, while the 2788cc had 170bhp which was good enough for 110-120mph top speed. This was an important, and successful, move for BMW and the sales results of the first two engine sizes led to a development of the range in 1971 with the 3.0S and three years later with the 3.3L. The 3 liter version of the six cylinder engine had been proved on the race track, and so it was a natural for the company's big sedan. The car was well received, additional performance (a top speed of 127mph and a 0-60mph of 8 seconds) were matched by improved handling and ventilated brakes. The performance aspect of the car really made it unmatched by any of its direct competitors. However, it was the introduction of the S-class Mercedes-Benz cars that forced the 3.3L version. Unlike the Mercedes it was not a completely new car but a stretched version of the existing one. The chassis became some four inches longer and the engine 300cc larger. Although the 3.3L was well-equipped and bigger, it was a shade heavier which meant that performance suffered a little when compared to the shorter 3.0S but this mattered less as the car was distinctly aimed at the chauffeur-driven prestige class. Any student of BMW's history cannot fail to recognise that the 3.3L represented a huge step forward from the time a mere dozen or so years before when the company was making funny looking small cars with two-stroke rear engines of only 697cc! This new determination to compete in the expensive luxury market has remained a highly important part of BMW's marketing strategy ever since and a succession of ever more sumptuous and sophisticated prestige automobiles have resulted to the delight of potential owners and motoring enthusiasts alike.

Left and above: The 2002 Turbo was produced primarily so that BMW could actually race the car internationally but was not an easy car to drive by any means, especially if it was raining! This beautifully-restored example is seen during a 1989 club race. In standard form the 1990cc slant four cylinder engine produced an impressive 170bhp.

Right: The BMW 2800 saw the company return to the luxury high performance big sedan section of the market. Six cylinder engines, injected from 1971, offered impressive performance. Disk brakes all round, power steering and limited slip differential were available.

BMW 2800CS/2.5CS/3.0CS/3.0CSL *1968-1975*

The Class Act

For this author at least, this model range is the beginning of what BMW represents today. These are the BMW coupes that remain to this day, the class act. They had, no that's incorrect – they still have – everything that makes a good sporting sedan; style, excellent performance and a motorsport reputation that many motoring managing directors would sell their balance sheets for. Yes, these models are impressive. The range started with the sedan version with two door coupe models always being a good sales option. That was the 2800CS and the 2.5CS, but it was when the racing tested 3 liter was installed that things began really to take off. These models ooze racing, the 3.0CSL being a lightweight coupe with a top speed in excess of 130mph and a 0-60mph time of just over seven seconds – and that was more than two seconds quicker than the comparable Mercedes-Benz 350SL! The 3.0CSi version of 1974 is now lovingly known as the 'Batmobile.' With its massive front air dam, roof spoiler and rear trunk-lid wing, this remains a stunning machine. Its looks were not to everyone's delight, however. When it was first introduced the German authorities banned its sale for public road use. Top speed was around 137mph and 0-60mph time was under seven seconds. The car handled like it looked, as a true racing thoroughbred. As you can read in the motorsport chapter of this book, it was as much of a sensation on the race track as it was on the road. There was only one criticism of the car and that was its price. Too expensive, the media claimed. If only they could have realised the value of the car a mere 15 years later. And anyway, you pay for class.

These pictures here represent examples of the beginning of BMW's modern style. The 1973 3.0 CSL (*left*) remains a highly distinctive sporting sedan. This range was successful on both the road and the race tracks of the world.

Below: This is the famous BMW 'Batmobile.' The extreme wing and spoiler combination were not just for show, they were aerodynamic aids necessary for the race track.

Below left: Inside too, the three spoke wheel and figure-hugging seats continue the car's motorsporting image. This is one serious motor car.

BMW 5 Series *1972-1981*

The New Generation

By the 1970s BMW could afford to breathe something of a corporate sigh and even allow itself a metaphorical pat on the back. Out of the red and into the black, the company had shown the quality of its product and sales responded. For the 1970s, however, there was no evidence of a company standing still. The new 5 Series, introduced in 1972, represented the start of a major rationalisation across the entire range. The 5 Series was the mid-size BMW, set to replace the 2500/2800/3.0 models. The difference was that there was now a 2 liter, four cylinder engine to complement the latest development of the famous straight six. The 1990cc engine was available in carburetor form, offering 115bhp or, with Kugelfischer mechanical fuel injection, 125bhp (later models used the improved Bosch K-Jetronic system). This engine was smooth and flexible — especially if compared to other four cylinder cars of the period — and opened up the model to a new market. Styling was not a radical change from before but was nevertheless distinctive. The range also included six cylinder versions which obviously offered the top performance; the 525 and 528 used Solex carburetors and the top of the range, the 528i, had the Bosch injection system and 177bhp. Suspension on all models was the by now familiar independent MacPherson strut front and independent trailing arm rear. Caution was to be advised when driving rapidly in the wet when the rear end would slide rather more easily than it should. For the first time, BMW introduced an M Sport version in the range with the M535i (see Chapter 3).

A major rationalisation across the entire range saw the announcement of the new BMW 5 Series in the early 1970s. The new four door sedans were available with a range of four and six cylinder engines, including the 528i (*below*) and the 525i (*right*).

BMW 3 Series *1975-1982*

Logical Development

BMW's rationalisation program moved from the mid-sized sedans down to the smaller models in 1975 when the very successful '02' model range was replaced with the new 3 Series. Bearing a strong family resemblance to its larger brother, the 3 Series had a hard act to follow as the previous small BMWs, the 2002 in particular, had been very popular. The 3 Series was, however, an improvement but there were significant links with the previous model. For instance, the 1573cc four cylinder engine that was fitted to the 316. The 318 had the 98bhp 1766cc unit and the other four cylinder models used the 1990cc four, both in carburetor and fuel injected form with 109bhp and 125bhp respectively. All models had the same two-door bodyshell. Perhaps the most significant move, however, came in 1977 when the 3 Series gained two versions of the six cylinder engine. In carburetor form it was not particularly exciting and it's arguable whether it was better than the injected four, but the more powerful 323i version held the BMW sporting small sedan flag high. The Bosch injected machine had 143bhp and impressive performance, 126mph top speed, 0-60mph in just over eight seconds. It also had handling to match, firm and enjoyable in the dry but with just that hint of spice in the wet when the rear end would bite back rather too easily due to that trailing arm rear suspension set up. There was even an open-topped version built for BMW by Baur in 1978.

The wind of change that blew through BMW's design department produced the 3 Series range in the mid 1970s. Bearing a strong resemblance to its larger brother, the initial production run was only available in two door form. Four door models were not introduced until the range was revamped in 1983.

Look at these pictures of the 635CSi and then turn back a few pages to the 3.0 CSL models that preceded it. The BMW 6 Series had all carried over all the necessary character of those earlier models while also being strikingly modern and reflecting the company's desire for a strong family resemblance to both the 3 and the 5 Series.

BMW 6 Series *1976-1989*

Carrying The Tradition

Taken in isolation, new model designs from any manufacturer can be accepted without full appreciation. When BMW announced the 6 Series in 1976, the company's careful and distinctive strategy was evident. Not only did the 6 Series have the strong family resemblance that was now obvious with both the 3 and the 5 Series, the new coupe also had the right links with the fabulous models it was replacing. Gone were all the aerodynamic appendages of the Batmobile stunners to be replaced with a svelte coupe which was no longer brash but no less sporting for that. As before, the coupe bodies were built by Karmann with final assembly at the wonderfully named Dingolfing factory in Bavaria. Appropriately all models had the six cylinder engine in different guises. Bottom of the range in the German market was the 630 CS with 'only' 185bhp. Export markets tended, as usual, to get different specification models. For the UK market, for example, the base model was the 628CSi (184bhp). Other versions were the 633CSi (200bhp), the 635CSi (218bhp) with the list topped by the exciting M635CSi introduced in 1984 with its four-valve per cylinder technology developed for the 3453cc engine and offering 286bhp, 160mph guided missile performance potential. As with the previous coupe models, the 6 Series has been a success both in the showroom and on the race tracks of Europe.

Left and below: Based on the styling of the coupe, the first range of 7 Series BMWs offered all the luxury, and that little extra space for adults in the rear! The 745i (shown here) had a 3.2 liter turbocharged power unit producing 252bhp. The 7 Series was the first model to feature ABS (anti-lock) brakes.

Right: It's spot the difference time. The second generation of 5 Series models hardly looked any different. This was a little misleading as much was changed in the production process making the car much lighter and a correspondingly better performer.

Above right: There is little visual difference to distinguish this 1987 M5 from its 5 Series cousins but performance, of course, was radically improved.

BMW 7 Series *1977-1986*

Top of The Nest

The design of the 6 and 7 Series was kept as common as possible to aid the production process. With the 7 Series models, however, the bodies were built in-house. This is the top of the BMW luxury range. Again, as you would probably expect by now, the model uses various versions of the six cylinder engine. Originally, fuel injection was only available for the top of the list 733i, but from 1979 all models had the smoothing benefit of Bosch L-Jetronic injection, as befitted such a range. With this announcement the family was complete; 3, 5, 6 and 7 series. What was most significant about these new models was that they really took BMW into the electronic computer age because, in the 732i, BMW had the first production car to be fitted with the new digital electronic management system from Bosch. Today, electronic engine management is an accepted, even expected, feature of luxury and high performance machines, but that should not take away any of the significance of this first introduction. Another significant first for this range of cars was the fitting of an ABS (anti-locking) brake system. The top performer among these models was the 745i which had a turbocharged version of the 3210cc engine developing 252bhp.

BMW 5 Series *1981-1987*

Spoilt for Choice?

The second version of the 5 Series was an interesting development for a number of reasons. Firstly it did not look significantly different from the previous model. Indeed, BMW described the change at the time as 'highly refined body design.' However, despite the fact that it looked like the previous one, it was very different and much improved; almost, dare we suggest, as if BMW was not happy with its first attempt and had another go. The similarity in the design was misleading as only the doors and the roof pressings remained from the previous model. The result was a much lighter car, with equally improved sound insulation which made for a more refined mid-range sedan. The range of engines available for this second 5 Series was extensive; four and six cylinder, an engine designed principally for fuel economy, six cylinder diesels, with and without turbochargers, and the M5 model. BMW had worked on the 528i's rear suspension and this model was certainly less prone to want to step out of line under power or when lifting off mid-corner. However, the rest of the range would have to wait until every model was so improved. Once again there was an M Sport model, this time called the M5 with its 3453cc, six cylinder engine offering 286bhp. One of the more interesting decisions with this new model was to produce an 'economy' version. The 525e was launched for the US and Japanese markets and had a high compression ratio (11.0:1) version of the 2.7 liter six cylinder with a small port cylinder head and long inlet tracks. It's a little unfair to call it an economy model and indeed the 'e' stood for 'eta' from the Greek expression meaning efficiency.

BMW 3 Series *From 1982*

Second Generation

After the second version of the 5 Series, there were no surprises when the second generation 3 Series cars emerged, looking rather similar to the original models. BMW said it was concentrating on consistently improving a successful product. One of the most obvious developments, however, was the much needed addition of a four door version; a move that much increased the market segment for the car. Driveline and engines were virtually unchanged and power outputs certainly remained as before. Once again, however, there had been subtle changes to the units; narrow crankshaft bearings, lighter valve springs, new crankshaft and transmission castings. All these developments were aimed at making an already impressive engine range even more refined and smoother. One very pleasing underbody change was seen at the rear. Like some of the second stage 5 Series models, the rear suspension set-up was altered with the angle of the semi-trailing arms reduced. This was a vast improvement and virtually eliminated the previous character criticism that BMWs have rather tricky handling on the limit. 1988 saw an important change with the introduction of a new 1.8 liter four cylinder engine. This particular engine was under development at the same time as the superb V12 unit that came for the next generation 7 Series and the 850i models. It was time for a change as the previous 1.8 liter engine could be traced back to the 1960s, this new model having more power (115bhp), better torque and better fuel efficiency.

BMW 325iX *From 1985*

Move to Four-wheel Drive

In the second half of the 1980s there has been an increasing move toward four-wheel drive cars. Obviously, BMW's engineers were aware of this — especially when one remembers that Audi, the true exponents of the four-wheel drive philosophy are not far away in Ingolstadt. It was no great surprise, therefore, when an all-wheel drive version of the popular and successful 325i was introduced in 1985. The system used was simple and well proven by other manufacturers (it's very similar to the system used by Ford of Europe). Power to the rear wheels is taken through a viscous coupling that has the effect of 'sharing' the amount of power between front and rear. The lock up nature of the coupling means that on normal, dry road conditions the power output is split with 63 percent going to the rear wheels, 37 percent to the front. If either set of wheels begins to slip due to a change in the surface (driving across intermittent snow or ice for instance) the viscous coupling is able to 'adjust' the drive that goes to each axle. Obviously having a permanent system like this does soak up a certain amount of engine power but the 325i's 170bhp still ensures that the 325iX is a brisk performer. This writer has made a number of cross-country trips in nasty weather and been most impressed by the grip and roadholding available during such adverse conditions. It is also impressive that BMW has avoided putting the script 'four-wheel drive' anywhere on the vehicle; only the X added discreetly to the usual badge tells the story.

Like the 5 Series, the second generation 3 Series models did not show a significant visual change. Evolution rather than revolution. The major change in the body was the availability of four doors.

Left: Inside, the now familiar simple but effective style of the BMW fascia. Large, clear instruments are neat and easy for the driver to read.

Above: The 325iX looks like any other BMW but it is significantly different under the skin. This is the four-wheel drive version of the 3 Series range, an exceptionally good car to drive in poor weather conditions.

BMW 325i Convertible *From 1986*

Fresh Approach

With the introduction of the revamped 3 Series, BMW had turned again towards its heritage to offer an open-topped model in its range. Coach-builders Baur of Stuttgart once again built a Cabriolet 3 Series BMW complete with a distinctive integral roll over bar. (They had previously built a convertible based on the 1500). This structure was far from just a visual addition since the main problem with a convertible version of any sedan is the potential loss of structural stiffness. With the roll-over bar fitted, much of the potential 'scuttle shake' – as the flexing of an open-topped body is called – can be eliminated. From spring 1986, however, BMW introduced its own open-topped convertible, a completely re-engineered model that did away with the need to have any unsightly roll-over bar and could therefore be a real convertible. BMW engineers had been impressed with the Baur Cabriolet but looked afresh at the whole problem and designed a completely new body-shell that had a great deal of extra steel to strengthen it; so much extra metal that despite not having all the weight of the roof and associated glass area, the convertible is some 290 pounds heavier than the sedan. The soft top was later given an electric motor to raise and lower it into position. In 1989 BMW offered a convertible version of the M3 in limited numbers built by Motor-sport.

BMW 7 Series *From 1986*

Electronic Wizardry

The new 7 Series range was introduced in 1986 and it's a sobering thought that the research and development program that went into the new range cost in excess of $1000 million. You'd expect an impressive range of machines for that and with the 7 Series you would not be disappointed. Looking like a larger 5 Series (or with the 5 Series being like a smaller 7, depending on how you see it) the family resemblance is there as are the impressive aerodynamics from the smooth body shape. The models are jam-packed with electronic details. Electronic systems control the engine, the anti-lock brakes, the anti-spin control, and the performance of the shock absorbers. The four speed automatic transmission has various driving pro-grams which alter when the transmission changes up and down. There are even memory functions on the electronic seat adjustment. The air conditioning is automatic as is the door lock de-icing. With all that on board, driving seems almost secondary. The 7 Series has three engine options: the 2986cc, 188bhp in the 730i; the 3430cc, 211bhp in the 735i and the V12 750i described separately. There are long wheelbase versions available, designated the L models and these offer 4.5 inches more legroom in the rear, obviously aimed at the chauffeur-driven sector of the market. With a car like this, however, it seems criminal to have one and not ache to drive it.

Above: Probably one of the most 'intelligent' mass produced cars ever built. The latest version of the 7 Series is packed with electronics. You name it, this car's got a button for it.

Left: The 325i Convertible is certainly an open-topped car for all conditions. The electronically operated power roof is so simple to operate and has the added advantage of remaining reasonably stylish when up.

Right: A three spoke steering wheel, usually reserved for the Sport versions, is used in the 325i Convertible.

BMW 750i *From 1987*

Six Are Best, Twelve Are Better

For a company that had such a reputation for its smooth and flexible six cylinder engines, the move to a new power unit was an important one. The V12 engine was the first by a German manufacturer for nearly 50 years and the first V12 engine to be fitted with a catalytic converter. (BMW's present range are fitted with catalytic converters in countries where these are required by law and this equipment is available as an option in other markets.) The 5 liter (4988cc) light alloy unit develops no less than 300bhp and 332 foot-pounds of torque. Electronic engine management systems control fuel injection, ignition and catalytic systems for the two rows of cylinders. With all that power, the BMW 750i and its long wheelbase cousin, the 750iL, is obviously a good performer despite being a large and relatively heavy machine. In acceleration it will reach 60mph in just over seven seconds and has a top speed of 155mph – at which point the electronics take over and govern the speed. In other words, the 750i is restrained from going any faster than 155mph! The V12 BMW is a delight to drive. For such a big car it is exceptionally nimble and with the automatic transmission switched to the 'Sport' mode it becomes a lively mover that makes cross-country journeys a breeze.

The BMW 750i is significant in that it has a new V12 engine under the hood. Producing no less than 300bhp the car has a restricted top speed, it will 'only' reach 155mph. Beautifully smooth, the 750i is a delight to drive. A large, extremely luxurious sedan that remains a 'driver's car.'

BMW first produced a Touring model back in 1971 based on the 02 Series. The latest version is based on the 3 Series and available with a number of engine options; 2 liter, turbo diesel, and 2.5 liter (shown here). It is also possible to have a four-wheel drive version.

BMW 325i Touring *From 1988*

What's in a name?

So, this is the station wagon version of the 3 Series . . . Hush your mouth, that's not a description that you will find in any BMW brochure. This is not a station wagon, it is merely the Touring version of the 325i. BMW has had a Touring model before, back in 1971 when it was a three door version of the 2002. In that model, however, the angle of the rear door could lead you to describe it as a hatchback. The new Touring has a rear door at far less of an angle . . . rather like you might see on a station wagon. That's enough of the smart gibes, the Touring is an excellent car, however you describe it. Based on the four door version of the 325i, the rear threequarters of the body has been extensively reworked – a necessity because of the removal of the rear bulkhead. This is the area in the sedan that adds to the car's excellent torsional stiffness so the engineers had to put additional bracing at both sill and window levels in the new model. The Touring is available with the 1990cc engine, the six cylinder turbocharged diesel unit offering 115bhp or in four-wheel drive format as the 325iX Touring.

When the latest 5 Series range was unveiled it received universal acclaim. A more rounded body style brought it right up to date, and although looking very similar to its bigger brother the 7 Series, this model does have a character of its own.

The range is very comprehensive from the 2 liter version up to the impressive 535i. All models feature versions of the injected six cylinder engine that has served BMW so well. The interior photograph (*bottom right*) shows a version fitted with the M Sport steering wheel.

BMW 5 Series *From 1988*

Five Star, No Question

Third time lucky? Hardly. This may be the third generation of the BMW 5 Series but you do not build a model range of this quality by luck; you do it with extensive research and development, an attention to detail, a pursuit of excellence and an in-built understanding of the indefinable quality that makes a good car. The styling enhances the corporate 'family' image and the 5 Series closely resembles the bigger 7 Series models. It is a very clean design with much improved aerodynamics. It is a significant step forward from the previous 5. Engines for the 5 Series are as you would expect, being versions of the six cylinder: the 520i with the 1990cc, 129bhp version; the 525i, 2494cc, 170bhp; the 530i, 2986cc, 188bhp and the 535i, 3430cc, 211bhp. There is also an 115bhp turbocharged diesel unit. All engines have the advanced Digital Motor Electronics engine management systems. Anti locking (ABS) brakes are also standard. Of course, it would not be a BMW without semi-trailing arm rear suspension but this too has been extensively reworked to include anti-dive and anti-squat geometry. In simple terms it means that the latest 5 Series handles extremely well both in the wet and the dry. The suspension can be tuned to suit the driver's moods from inside the car. The 5 Series models are fitted with Electronic Damper Control which allows the driver to alter the ride due to the variable shock absorber control; normal, sports and comfort are available. Top of the 5 Series range is the exceptional M5 model built by Motorsport.

BMW 850i *From 1990*

Ultimate Coupe

At the end of 1989, BMW caused quite a sensation at the Frankfurt Motor Show by unveiling the 850i, the company's superb V12-engined coupe. This beautiful looking machine is the natural replacement to the 635 CSi and continues BMW's desire to have an exclusive coupe model in its range. The first models have the 300bhp V12 engine, which like the 750i is fitted with an electronic governor to restrict the top speed to 'only' 155mph. It is thought that unrestricted the 850i would be capable of in excess of 180mph. Besides the obvious attractions of the new bodyshape, BMW used the 850i to show its new integral five link axle set-up for the rear suspension. BMW is also going to build an open-topped convertible version of the 850i. This exciting development is in direct competition to Mercedes-Benz and that company's new SL convertible. The range will also be widened to include 12 valve 3 liter and 24 valve 3.5 liter models using the same specification engines that have been so successful in the 7 Series. As you might expect, the 850i is packed with hi-tech electronics including tire pressure sensors, anti-lock brakes, anti-wheel spin equipment, electrically adjustable seats and integral seat belts (essential for the clean lines of the convertible). This model is an apt place to end this particular section of the book. Quite simply, the 850i has to be the most desirable BMW ever built.

Launched just as this book was being written, the 850i shows the direction BMW will take into the 1990s. Fitted with the 300bhp V12 engine, shown *right*, the 850i is the natural replacement for the old 6 Series. With a new convertible version on the books, BMW is still producing dream machines.

M Sport: Mouth-watering

These are the elite. Simply put, they represent a design and development that takes already high quality prestige motor cars into a new class. Even more simply put, these cars are special.

The M Sport range is a natural extension of the company's automotive philosophy. BMW has had a strong history of performance machinery designed to be successful in motorsport. Right from the early 1930s, the company produced special versions of the 315 and 319 models. From these came the 328 and the famous Mille Miglia winning coupe version. The difference between those early days and now is that for the 1990s, marketing, packaging and promotion of a product is far more overt; you don't just build special performance versions of your cars, you shout about the fact. And that impression is fully endorsed when you open the hood of any of these models; plastered across the engine cover are the words BMW M POWER.

The M, naturally, stands for Motorsport, an activity that BMW has been successful in for many, many years and that story is fully documented elsewhere in this book. What the reader needs to recognise now, however, is that all BMW motorsporting developments and the M Sport car production must always be thought of together.

BMW Motorsport GmbH was started in 1972 and with just eight employees could justifiably call itself Germany's 'smallest car company.' Motorsport is a division of BMW AG and has grown to have its own production plant facilities at Garching, just outside Munich. Motorsport now employs a total of just over 400 people, split between the racing engine and development works at Preussenstrasse at Munich and the much larger Garching plant.

It's quite logical that the first M Sport model should be designated the M1 – it is equally logical that the car should have been designed and built for the purpose of both motorsport and as an exclusive, extremely fast road car. The history of the M1 is, however, far from simple.

Obviously at the beginning, the Motorsport department could not just design and build a completely new car, the investment in the facilities for such a project would be enormous for such a small offshoot of the main company. As the concept was for a mid-engined two-seater sports car it was a logical step to work with those masters of that particular design specification; the Italians. BMW had the M1's body design done by Giorgio Giugiaro's ItalDesign of Turin. The plan was to have the cars built at Lamborghini's Santa Agata factory with the engine and transmissions shipped there from BMW in Germany. Given BMW's experiences with financial problems it is ironic but, one can say with the benefit of hindsight, ultimately beneficial that Lamborghini should find itself in dire financial straits and unable to complete the deal with BMW. The problems also meant that the M1 had a very protracted birth. Its original inception was in 1975 but the first prototypes did not turn a wheel until 1977 with the first production version being shown at the 1978 Paris Motor Show.

The car was the brain-child of BMW Motorsport boss – and successful touring car racer – Jochen Neerpasch who wanted to build a potential racing winner conceived from scratch to meet the racing regulations then in force. The BMW philosophy that success on the track would ensure sales on the road would continue. The debacle with Lamborghini made it look like this would never happen but thankfully, if a little belatedly, production began.

Previous page: The BMW M3 was built to win on the track and delight on the road, a classic sporting sedan of the 80s.

Below and right: The M1 was the first M Sport car. It had a protracted birth since the car was to be built by Lamborghini but turned out to be pure BMW. The six cylinder power unit was placed behind the front two seats in the classic mid-engine position.

Below right: Open the hood and it says it all. . . This is the four cylinder, 2.3 liter unit in the M3.

Left: This is chassis number 19 of one of the rarest and, many would say, most desirable BMWs ever built.

Above left and right: This M1 is fitted with non-standard wheels, these coming from the German manufacturer BBS. A rare and extremely valuable machine.

The glassfiber body panels, there were 10 in all, came from Italy to the Stutt-gart-based coachbuilders Baur who assembled the whole cars with the mechanical parts obviously coming from BMW. The completed cars were then taken to BMW Motorsport for tuning and road testing before being offered for sale. As the motorsport career of this car and its own racing series are dealt with in the appropriate chapter, here we will concern ourselves with the road-going version; the first M Sport road car.

The body design was stunning and noticeably understated, a trait which can be seen on some of the latest M Sport models. Nearly 15 years after it was first conceived, it is far from outdated. For cars, however, looks are not everything and in the case of the M1 it had just the engine to match the visual appeal. Based on the production six cylinder block, the 3453cc power unit boasted four valves per cylinder with fuel injection. These hand-built engines gave 277bhp at 6500rpm (in racing form the same engine could be tuned to over 470bhp!) and a healthy 239 foot-pounds of torque at 5000rpm. Independent suspension of wishbone and coil spring type was the ideal set up to allow the frequent adjustment necessary for top class racing while offering exceptional handling and road-holding in ordinary use.

The reader should not get the impression that this is a highly strung racer with license plates. The M1 represents the philosophy that has continued throughout the M Sport program. The quality of the build is as good as any mass produced BMW. The M1, for instance, had electric window lifts, a reasonable amount of space for weekend luggage and a full stereo system. The engine would tick over at a burbling 800rpm and the car could happily be driven through city traffic. Move the needle up through the range to 4500rpm and the M1 would pull like a train. It didn't have quite the midrange torque of a comparable Ferrari V12 or Aston Martin V8 engine, but the multi-valve six cylinder engine would effectively deliver the performance goods when properly driven. The performance figures against the clock back this up; 0-60mph in only 5.5 seconds and a top speed of 162mph.

That kind of ability doesn't just fade away with the passage of time and with only just over 400 M1s ever built, the present day value is high. If you wanted one, as this is being written in late 1989, a good M1 would set you back around $120,000 plus. That's more than twice the original 'list price.'

While it took rather a long while to arrive, and in retrospect didn't remain in production for that long, the M1 was an excellent start for the fledgling Motorsport department's road car production. Today, the division can justifiably call itself a car producer, the Garching plant actually building 2500 units in 1989 — and that is far from satisfying the demand.

Walk around the M Sport premises today and you are struck by a number of things; it is clean, neat and tidy and is unlike any modern car manufacturing facility, much more like a hi-tech motorsport workshop. Indeed, that is effectively what it really is, the only difference being that when the cars leave Garching, they go on the road not the track. When this writer visited the premises in 1989, the entire production was concentrated on the new M5 model. Earlier in the year — before the summer — they had built around 100 M3 convertibles and 300 M635CSi coupes (the last of these to be made).

Fully built body monocoques (effectively a fully trimmed shell) are received direct from BMW AG. They are then washed and inspected before all the suspension, running gear and that all-important engine is fitted. The attention to detail is obvious at every aspect of the build, and the care taken by the specially selected and trained mechanics results in some beautifully built machines. When I wanted to photograph one of the M5 engine bays there was a great commotion while a small piece of brown sticky tape was removed from the matt black engine cover. After the photograph had been taken, the tape was replaced. The reason? On the under-side of the engine cover there was a small half-inch scratch, temporarily protected by the tape. Difficult to see with the naked eye, this had been found during the final inspection and would be repaired before this car was delivered to its new owner. That's what you are paying for perhaps, but it's still impressive.

Above right: Like all M3s, this British-registered example is left hand drive.

Left and right: The latest M5 model is the epitome of German conservatism. The small M Sport badge on the front grille, the twin tail exhaust pipes and the alloy wheels are the only visual differences from the standard car. The performance, however, is significantly different. This is an express train on wheels.

Left: The understated elegance of the M5.

Right and below left: One could never say that the BMW M3 is a subtle and understated machine. The body style screams raw power. The ultimate 'boy racer's' machine? Not really, this car has performance and handling characteristics to match those looks.

But that attention to detail is not half as impressive as the car itself. The M5 is the latest in the M Sport family tree and it still has a link with the original M1 in that it uses a development of that first engine. Still in straight six cylinder format, the multi-valve and fuel injected unit now has the aid of different camshaft profiles and the mechanical miracles of a modern electronic engine management system which means the M5 produces no less than 315bhp at a roaring 6900rpm with 360 foot-pounds of torque at a relatively high 4750rpm.

Changes have understandably also been made to the suspension set-up when compared to the standard 5 Series BMW. Front and rear spring rates are stiffer, there are different front dampers from the standard car and the front and rear anti-roll bars are thicker. The whole car is 20mm (0.8inch) lower. ABS (anti-lock) brakes are fitted as standard, while the brake disks are larger and the fronts are inner-ventilated. The rear axle is self-leveling (in other words the suspension learns to cope with whatever weight is at the rear, whether the car is empty or has a full complement of passengers and their luggage). A limited slip differential with a 25 percent lock-up ability is fitted to ensure the best traction capabilities when the car is accelerating on difficult surfaces.

The model is based on the latest 5 Series BMW and at first glance it may not be easy to tell the M5 apart from its lesser cousins. That is all part of the understated policy that we have mentioned before. There are two discreet 'M5' badges fore and aft, it has twin exhaust pipes and each M5 comes with a unique set of light alloy wheels that are sculptured not only for their looks but for their ability to direct air on to the brakes to aid cooling. Apart from that it all looks the same, until that is, you get behind the wheel.

M Sport personnel enthuse that no two M5s are the same. They are all sold before they are built and the new owners are encouraged to choose from a variety of extras, whether it be for the complete full leather interior trim treatment, car phone, custom designed 12 channel stereo system or highly sophisticated anti-theft device. The choice is up to the – lucky – new owner who is actively encouraged to go to the workshop and see the car being built – try asking if that is possible after ordering your new Ford.

For the driver, the M5 offers a level of indulgence that is available in few

other motor cars presently built; certainly there is not another four door sedan to match it. A special M Sport steering wheel – leather trimmed of course – and matching gearshift – with its shift pattern and the two bar red and blue Motorsport stripes illuminated, of course – are the only visual differences from a standard 5 Series BMW. Potter off into town traffic and the smooth, svelte style that you can transport yourself about in is pleasurable if slightly soporific. What is all the fuss about? Stop at traffic lights on a German slip road and see the light gray color of the forthcoming Autobahn stretch towards the horizon, match full throttle acceleration with 7200rpm change up points and the M5 will transport you to that horizon very rapidly indeed. If you want tire squealing decibels and coarse acceleration that forces you back in the seat, then don't buy an M5. This machine offers almost sublime acceleration, something that feels as one might imagine time travel, while being almost arrogant in its efficiency. If you want to travel fast in this car, very fast, then don't expect to impress your passengers, chances are they will not even realise what is happening. The ultimate driving machine is the way BMW describe these cars. Well, it is difficult to know if that is really the case, but it must be close.

Bearing all that in mind, it is not surprising to hear that the M Sport department has had to increase its projected production quota of this car. Initially only 1500 were due to be built but the demand has been so high that that figure was soon forgotten and that was even before they even started offering right hand drive versions for the UK market!

If, as BMW's marketing department would have you believe, the M5 is for the successful businessman who wants the best but doesn't want to drive an overtly ostentatious machine, then all drivers of M3s must be brash young things indeed. That is perhaps a little unfair, but the visual appeal of the M3 is far from subtle and understated; this is one brazen motor car. And so it should be, because like the M1 before, it was designed directly for the race track. The M5 is unlikely ever to have a competition program due to the fact that international regulations mean that you would need to build 5000 in one year – a total that would require a great deal of investment and not be possible with the present set up at Garching. Also, if there were 5000 M5s, this would also dilute the exclusive tag of the car. The M3, however, was aimed

Left: The BMW M3 is only available in left-hand drive form. And only available suitably badged *(right* and *below).*

Below right: The BMW M535i offered competent drivers a lot of excitement. Not as refined as the latest M5, it will still out-perform many an Italian sports car.

directly at a successful racing career, with the quality of the road car being an important, but secondary, consideration.

Building a car specifically to compete on the race track is not a new idea; many manufacturers do it. These cars are often called homologation specials, the words referring to the fact that a specific number of road versions have to be built to allow the model to meet — to be homologated for — international sporting regulations. In the past, some of these cars have been nothing more than racing cars with extra seats, carpets and a stereo system. In other words while they are certainly exciting, they are often not cars you could live with day-to-day. That was not the way the BMW wanted the M3. It was to be a winner on the track while also having the same high quality as a road car that people had come to expect from BMW. The M3 achieved both.

Based on the 3 series the M3 has the aggressive stance to stir all red-blooded males (and a goodly number of females too!). The bodywork changes are not just for looks, however, as they were made for important reasons. The bulging wheel arches allow a wider wheel and tire combination for racing, up to 10 inches wide being possible. The front air dam has scoops that aid cooling to the front brakes when the car is raced. The rear window is raked an extra three degrees and the trunk lid raised by 40mm to channel air over the rear spoiler and add to the car's down-force (this is the aerodynamic effect which, literally, pushes the rear of the car down to give extra traction).

The suspension changes on the M3 are comprehensive. M Sport's head of engineering, Thomas Ammerschlager, worked long and hard at this to ensure it would be right for road and track. The front castor angles are all changed to give the car more feel through the steering, special M3 stub axles have tougher wheel bearings from the 5 Series range and provision of a thicker anti-roll bar completes the changes at the front. At the rear, the design is closer to the standard 3 Series but it gets the all important limited slip differential and stiffer anti roll bar.

When it came to the engine, logic would have perhaps dictated that M Sport go to work on the smooth straight six that nestles under the 325i's hood. But no. That was simply not good enough. M Sport wanted an engine that would rev to a higher limit and therefore developed a new engine based on the four cylinder block that was the 1500cc heart of Nelson Piquet's Brab-

ham Formula One car that won the 1983 World Championship. Another way of looking at it, in crude engineering terms, is that the M3's 2303cc four cylinder is two thirds of the six cylinder engine of the M1. Twin Cams and a Bosch Motronic engine management system allow a racing unit to rev to 9000rpm, with a screaming 10,000rpm available at times. All this means that the road driver has 200bhp at a glorious sounding 6750rpm (the race cars give no less than 330bhp) with 177 foot-pounds of torque coming in at 4750rpm. The performance figures quote 0-60mph in under 7 seconds and a top speed of 143mph. Those figures tell you much about what it is like to drive the M3 — but it is totally the opposite to the M5.

Keep an M3 below about 4000rpm and you won't be impressed. Fail to master the awkward gear shift with its racing selection of a 'dog-leg' first gear and the M3 may disappoint. If that happens then listen for the mechanical snigger that will undoubtedly come from the engine as you walk away ready to hand the keys back to the dealer. Remember why this car was built and drive it accordingly and you'll never hand the keys over to anyone. Keep the

engine running between 4000rpm and the road car's 7250rpm electronic cut-out, be precise but firm with your gearchanges and learn to be in the right ratio at the right time and the M3 meets the simple definition of a driver's car. No stunning acceleration, perhaps, but the kind of point to point cross country times that you should certainly keep to yourself. Despite its aggressive looks, you don't boast with an M3, you just drive it. Yes, this is one of my favorite cars.

In keeping with the M Sport philosophy, there are development versions of the M3 that can make it different from the, albeit relatively small, M3 crowd. Johnny Cecotto has been one of the top competition drivers in a BMW M3 and there is a special 'Cecotto M3' available (in Britain it is known as the Roberto Ravaglia M3 in recognition of that driver's World and European Touring Car Championship victories). With the aid of different camshaft profiles and a tweak in the engine management system, an extra 15bhp is available. This increases the car's top speed to a cool 150mph and the 0-60mph acceleration comes down to 6.5seconds. The car's body has a slightly deeper front spoiler and altered rear fenders. Plus, under the hood, the engine is painted the same color as the bodywork — and when that's bright red it makes for one impressive engine bay!

For BMW to be able to compete with the M3 in international motorsport, 5000 models had to be built within a 12 month production period. Production began in 1986 and to date, a total of 14,124 models have been sold, all of them in left hand drive form — the angle of the engine means that the complex exhaust system does not allow any space for a right hand drive steering column. As for the Cecotto M3s, only 505 of these have been produced so far.

When you have fully appreciated the M3's character, it is perhaps a little difficult to understand the philosophy behind the M3 convertible. Four seater convertibles have a high prestige value and this together with the build quality does make the 'standard' 3 series convertible very desirable, but who wants an open-topped race car? The answer has to be in the double character that the M3 has; you can cruise with a complement of passengers when the sun shines, while inwardly smiling at what the car could do if you really wanted it to.

The attention to detail is what you pay for, and it is what you get. As these photographs clearly show, the build quality of any M Sport model is extremely high and the sporting treatment extends from the exterior bodywork to the bucket seats and special steering wheel.

It's rather easier to understand the philosophy behind the remaining two M Sport models that have to be mentioned. The M535i that was introduced in 1984 was more than just an improvement on the standard 535i model, it was a revelation by comparison. When compared with the previous 5 Series range which were rather lackluster, the introduction by BMW's arch rivals Mercedes Benz of the new 190E 2.3 16 valve was a threat the Munich company could not take lying down. Again, the hand of Motorsport boss Jochen Neerspach can be seen because it was he who recognised the potential of using parts from the then top of the standard range 635CSi in the smaller, and therefore lighter, 5 Series bodyshell. The engine, therefore was the 3.5 liter six cylinder but in single overhead cam format. With L-Jetronic fuel injection the M535i had 218bhp, a 0-60mph acceleration in a fraction over seven seconds and a top speed of 143mph. The particular 5 Series that this model was based on had a rather less than perfect suspension set up, especially at the rear, and was quite capable of catching the less experienced

driver unprepared with its tail-happy handling. The M535i was better, but the trait was not completely cleared. A quick car no doubt, but one that needed skill and not a little respect under certain conditions.

The M635CSi is even quicker because the version of the six cylinder under its long hood is much closer in specification to the M1 that started the whole M Sport business. Four valves per cylinder and twin overhead cams gave the car 286bhp, an output that is above the original M1 (in road going trim) due largely to improvements in digital electronic engine management systems. Add to this the fact that the M1 had a compression ratio of 9.0 to 1 while the M635CSi was raised to 10.5 to 1. Stiffer springs and thicker anti roll bars uprated the car's suspension. Massive ventilated brakes are fitted to the front with the rear setup also being improved. Performance takes the car to 60mph in just over six seconds and to 100mph in under 18 seconds, when you have to change up to fourth gear! A top speed of 158mph speaks volumes for a car first produced in 1984.

There has only ever been one question held against the M635CSi. On paper, and on the road, it had the potential to be a formidable race car (BMW already raced versions of the 635CSi coupe). Quite why it was never produced in enough quantity to homologate for motorsport purposes is something of a mystery for enthusiasts. Motorsport did, however, produce a total of 5855 models over the car's five year production span.

That is the story of the M Sport BMWs, the elite of an already impressive range. Special cars yes, but built to the same high standards of all production BMWs. When you look at the performance potential of the latest M5 model the only question that remains is, what next? There seems little more that could be possible. Stretching the imagination, one wonders what would happen if Motorsport were to work its magic on the company's fabulous new V12 engine used in the top of the range models of the 7 Series and the latest BMW 850i. Or maybe if the sleek, almost cheeky, Z1 sports car was to find its way to the M Sport headquarters and be fitted with an M3 engine you could turn an already good car into a better one. Only time will tell what is to come next.

The M may officially stand for Motorsport, but surely mouth-watering is more appropriate?

Above: This is the power unit in the M535i. Not quite such an impressive sight as latter-day M Sport cars, but it's how it performs that counts.

Right: The M635 CSi looked ideally suited for the race tracks of Europe but surprisingly perhaps was never built in enough numbers to be eligible for competition. In total, only 5855 were built over a seven year period.

The BMW M635 CSi was extremely popular in the United Kingdom. Always a market that wants coupe versions, the M Sport model was something that appealed to the British sense of driving enjoyment.

Left and right: The impressive sight of the 286bhp six cylinder fuel injected engine, both out of and – squeezed – into the car.

Alpina: BMW's Alter Ego

If there is one single theme running through this book, it is that BMW makes exceptional sporting automobiles. Style, quality and performance are tags that only begin to describe what it is about BMW that raises the cars so high. It may come as something of a surprise, therefore, to find out that there is one man who is sure that he can improve on them. And if that is a surprise, then the fact that BMW happens to agree with, and completely supports, these claims is nothing short of a revelation. But then, Burkard Bovensiepen is a rather special man and his Alpina BMWs are rather exceptional cars.

Once destined to take over his father's typewriter business, Burkard Bovensiepen is now one of the world's most respected independent tuners and his involvement a further indication of the character of BMW cars. He is also one of Germany's biggest wine dealers, but more of that later.

The Alpina story starts back in the 1950s and 60s with Bovensiepen being groomed to lead the family business of producing typewriters. The problem was that the young Bovensiepen had developed a passion for fast cars. At this time, after-market tuning was big business in many other countries but disapproved of by German manufacturers. Bovensiepen believed this could be changed if the cars produced attempted to be better built than the manufacturers'. In other words he was convinced that he could produce tuned cars that the respective manufacturers would fully approve of. To this end he persuaded his father to allow him to develop a number of tuning kits – at first working on Fiats – with Alpina typewriters covering the costs. The important landmark in the story has to be the 1961 Frankfurt Motor Show and the announcement of the new BMW 1500. This small, compact sedan with its new four cylinder engine was eminently tunable. He took the new model and in twin carburetor form produced 92bhp which increased the car's top speed by 5mph up to 98mph and sliced seconds off the acceleration. It was an impressive start. Bovensiepen's love affair with the BMW began.

By 1965 the typewriter company had been sold and Bovensiepen had decided to set up his own tuning concern specialising in BMWs. In that first year the Alpina factory (Alpina was the name of his father's company) employed only six people and had a turnover of some $500,000. Today, Alpina employs over 100 people and the turnover is now measured in millions.

Much of the success of Alpina has been due to the fact that Bovensiepen has been able to develop a strong relationship with the manufacturer. This has not only given him a much needed secure financial base but it has also provided him with a well established network through which to market his cars; you can buy an Alpina BMW through any of the manufacturer's official dealerships, and that is the all-important stamp of approval.

The important thing to realise about these tuned models is that they are far from 'bolt-on' conversions and much more a product from a company that hand builds its own vehicles. BMWs arrive at the Buchloe factory unregistered and still in their protective wax. Customers don't just supply their cars for modification by Alpina, you actually buy a brand new Alpina model. Indeed, every car that leaves the factory carries a plaque on the fascia showing the Alpina crest – a neat heraldic shield showing a carburetor and crankshaft – and the car's individual build number. Bovensiepen describes the work that Alpina does to production BMWs as 're-engineering' rather than any more tacky description of tuning or converting.

The connection between Alpina and BMW is now so strong, that Bovensiepen is party to a great deal of information regarding future models and future research. Bovensiepen does, for instance, preview future models a long time before they are launched and this allows him to plan his own developments. In return, Alpina undertake always to tell the manufacturer what they are doing on the engineering front for any new model.

The engineering genius that is Alpina is based strongly on work done on the race track where the company has prepared racing BMWs for many years. The high point of this racing work must undoubtedly have been when Nelson Piquet took third place at the South African Grand Prix to win the

Previous page: It's hard to look at these cars and remember that the man who produced them used to make typewriters!

Left and right: The Alpina badging and the bodystyles have become more subtle in later years. This early Alpina B9 3.5 has the famous pin-striping and frontal spoiler treatment that is not to everyone's taste.

Left: The German conversion specialist doesn't leave the changes restricted to just the body work and the engine. He leaves his mark inside, too.

Right and below right: Based on the new 5 Series, the latest Alpina B10 has had a much more subtle visual treatment and its appearance is much the better for it.

1983 Formula One World Championship for Brabham-BMW. Why? Because much of the development of the four cylinder turbocharged engine that took Piquet to the title was done in the engine shop and dynamometer bays of Alpina Burkard Bovensiepen AG. Such a program was naturally kept very secret until BMW engineers themselves were satisfied that the engine was good enough and then took the program back to the company's own workshops in Munich. Alpina had done the groundwork, BMW would then take the Championship. Alpina was a good choice for all the initial development because the company has extensive knowledge of turbocharging, a fact obvious from the model range. That particular statement may seem a little dated when one considers that many manufacturers – including BMW – have over the last ten years or so turned away from the turbo and developed what could be described as more complex multi-valve engines. For Alpina, however, the turbocharged engine has certain advantages, one of them being the ever-more-stringent emission and noise laws that are being imposed across Europe. Germany and Switzerland especially have very severe noise level regulations and of course the turbocharged engine can be designed to produce large amounts of extra power with the only addition to the decibel level being the emotive whoosh and whistle of the power unit's turbine. Multi-valve engines by comparison tend to be much louder as they generally produce their maximum power outputs at much higher rpm limits.

In today's ever more cautious environment, emission laws for motor vehicles are being tightened and when that is looked at in isolation, it could be thought to be tolling the end of the high performance conversion. Bovensiepen is obviously aware of this and in the early 1980s started the significant program of developing Alpina's own catalytic converter-equipped cars. (Such equipment, of course, is now legally required in the USA, West Germany and Switzerland.) To enable the company to do this, Alpina had to invest in excess of Dm1 million to build its own exhaust emission laboratory. This has given Alpina the ability to develop powerful new engines that meet, and in many cases, exceed the necessary exhaust emission requirements.

The engineering philosophy at Alpina follows the route that tuning necessitates extra cubic capacity. And for this, of course, Alpina has an excellent starting point with the BMW six cylinder block. But tuning a modern car is far more than just giving it more umphh. Modern cars, especially cars of BMW's quality, are produced to a finite package with the car's performance matched to the way it handles and the way it rides. Alter one of these and you can upset that balance and ruin a car. Alpina is well aware of this necessity and that is never more obvious than on Alpina B11. Based on the 735i or 735iSE, there are only subtle changes to BMW's iron block six cylinder. The

two valve per cylinder head is modified, Mahle pistons are fitted and the lubrication system uprated with the addition of an oil cooler. By reprogramming the Bosch Motronic engine management system, the B11 engine has a 40bhp hike over the standard model's rating, raising it to 260bhp. To cope with this, the suspension has been altered with Bilstein gas shock absorbers and Alpina's own springs fitted all round. Attractive light alloy wheels are fitted; the rims being 8.5 inches at the front and a massive 10 inches at the rear. Shod with 235/45 front and 265/40 at the rear the B11 has a massive footprint on the road. But unlike the tires, the remainder of the B11 is far from low profile, fitted as it is with what can be described as the standard Alpina bodykit treatment, a deep front spoiler. The familiar Alpina pin-striping down the sides is also an option.

The package provides the standard 735i with sports car-like agility and stunning acceleration; the B11 will clock 60mph in 4.5 seconds and remember this car weighs 1.7 tonnes! The B11, while still resembling the 735i on which it is based, is actually a completely different car and an absolute joy for the pilot.

For the C2 Alpinas, based on the BMW 325i, the engine work is rather more extensive and aptly demonstrates the detail that goes into the re-engineering. The 325i engine is completely stripped and fitted with a longer throw crankshaft which increases the capacity of the ETA block to 2693cc, hence the C2 2.7 badging. Again a reworked cylinder head and Mahle pistons are fitted as is a completely new exhaust system. This results in a power increase of well over 20 percent with the car now having some 210bhp on tap, a 0-60mph acceleration time of under seven seconds and a top speed of over 140mph. The subtle suspension changes are similar to those on the B11 with the inclusion of Bilstein shock absorbers and stiffer Alpina springs all round. The familiar deep front spoiler and Alpina light alloy wheels are the only tell-tale sign for the casual observer and indeed, inside the car the layout is even more low key with just an Alpina steering wheel and special gearshift different from the standard car. Super acceleration and safe handling make this a very desirable motor car, especially the version based on the 325i Touring – a conversion that seems to appeal to the British market. In Sytner of Nottingham, Britain has the only Alpina dealer world-wide who is authorised to build Alpina cars, although once again they can be ordered direct through any official BMW dealer in the UK. Frank Sytner has a reputation for BMWs and regularly competes in British saloon car racing in a BMW M3.

And it is the M3 that has enticed Alpina back to the race track to build its own versions for the German Touring Car Championship, with one of the cars driven by Bovensiepen's son Andy. The cars are obviously built to conform to

Left: A discreet badge and molding on the air dam are the only identification at the front of this B10.

Right and below: It is possible to have the Alpina treatment on most of the models in the BMW range. The only restriction is your cheque book. This selection shows the Alpina Convertible and the Alpina Touring — more power and more space.

seems to be an emphatic yes, as the late 1989 launch of the Alpina B12, based on the V12 engine only goes to emphasise. As we have described elsewhere in this book, the 750i is the first model fitted with the V12 engine and is restricted to a maximum top speed of 155mph. When it is given the Alpina treatment, that speed goes up to an impressive 176mph! This is done by completely stripping the V12 and equipping it with a pair of Garrett turbo-chargers. Again Mahle pistons are used, with the compression ratio raised from 8.8:1 to 9.5:1. The engine's cylinder heads are reworked with over-sized valves. The result, according to Alpina, raises the standard car's 300bhp to 350bhp at only 5300rpm. Torque is increased in a similar grand manner up from 332 foot-pounds to 347 foot-pounds which arrives 100rpm earlier than standard at 4000rpm. With uprated chassis and suspension modifications the completed car would set you back well in excess of $100,000.

But where does the wine come into the equation? Back in the early 1970s Bovensiepen started dealing in wine. Today, the Alpina name makes him the biggest German dealer in wines from the Bordeaux region of France. Indeed, under the Alpina workshops is a beautifully designed cellar, kept at exactly the right temperature, where Bovensiepen keeps all his rarest vintages. The Alpina wine stock is huge and extra warehouses have had to be built with the company having more money invested in wine than in car spare parts. And while the car parts are completely turned over within the space of 12 months, the wine often takes a good deal longer – and gets correspondingly more valuable.

Drinking and driving do mix when it comes to Alpina. Good wine and exceptionally good cars. The only important difference is that, as Bovensiepen is known to comment, while it's all a matter of good taste, you drive the car first!

the necessary Group A regulations with all the parts coming from BMW Motorsport. Not surprisingly Bovensiepen strips all the cars down and re-builds them 'the Alpina way' and he is adamant that his cars are very different from other Group A BMW M3s. The racing side is only a small part of the Alpina business, but racing is very good for the image, as BMW itself knows.

The future? Can Burkard Bovensiepen continue to build ever more powerful versions of BMW sedans, especially when the mother company has its own very specialised department doing just that at M Sport? The answer

Motorsport:
A Race Apart

It wouldn't be possible any other way. Let's face it, no manufacturer could build high performance cars without being a devout believer in motorsport. There is no stronger test for a machine, or a manufacturer, than the race circuits of the world; no stronger test and no better endorsement of the product. And it was endorsement that really got BMW started in the first place.

In the 1920s, motorsport was not quite the glamor game that is seen today. Publicising your product was somewhat different; there was no television of course, no glossy magazine advertisements and certainly no newsstand shelves full of motoring magazines to publish rave reports about your cars. Motorsport was the only way to prove your product to the public. For BMW, motorsport has been a success right from the start.

Immediately the company acquired the rights to build the little Dixi, three of the 3/15PS models carrying the blue and white symbol for the first time entered the 1929 Austrian Alpine Trial. Driven by Buchner, Kandt and Wagner the marque took outright victory. The event was a tough performance test for the cars as it included driving over the Alpine passes and so success like this did much to emphasise the durability of these BMWs. Reliability was really what was needed in international motorsport at the time and this was no better emphasised than two years later when BMW entered a mammoth 10,000km rally which was a round trip to and from Berlin via France, Spain, Portugal, Italy, Yugoslavia, and Austria. A three car works team of 750cc, 18bhp Dixis continued BMW's success with victory once again.

The first real racing successes had to wait until after the introduction of the new six cylinder engines in 1933. Three brand new 315 BMWs won their class in the 1934 German Rally. This can really be seen as the first all-BMW model and is, therefore, the start of the real BMW motorsport story.

The 315 had the 1490cc version of the six cylinder engine punching out 40bhp. This was supplemented in 1935 by the 319 which had the 55bhp version of the now larger capacity 1911cc. Both these models took a multitude of class victories in various forms of motorsport and established the name of BMW as a competitive force. Indeed, it was the team prize for the 1934 Alpine Trial for the 315 that led to BMW's association with Frazer Nash, a British company that already had a good motorsport reputation and was impressed enough with the German machines to want to import them.

BMW really hit the headlines in Germany when the new two seater sports car, the 328, debuted in the 1936 Eifelrennen at the Nurburgring, the very heart of German motorsport. Despite the model still being more than two months away from the dealers' showrooms, Ernst Henne (who had already made his name breaking world records on two-wheeled BMWs) took the new 2 liter 328 to victory by a country mile. Victory at the Nurburgring was just the start. The 1971cc ohv engine developing 80bhp and capable of pushing the lightweight BMW to the magical 100mph, meant that BMW effectively made the 2 liter class its own preserve for several years. Up until the outbreak of the hostilities of World War II, BMW 328s were victorious at the British Tourist Trophy (the premier British touring car race and one that BMW has won as recently as 1987 with the M3), the Bucharest Grand Prix, the AVUS, the Grand Prix des Frontières, the Francorchamps 24 Hours, the German Grand Prix, the Tobruk-Benghazi-Tripoli, the Le Mans 24 Hours and the Italian classic the Mille Miglia. Right across Western Europe, therefore, the blue and white symbol collected the spoils. Bear in mind the relative inex-

Previous page: Roberto Ravaglia took the Schnitzer prepared BMW M3 to the 1987 World Touring Car Championship.

The BMW 315 (*above*) and 319 (*above right*) took a great number of class victories – and are still used in classic motor sport today. But it was the 328 (*left* and *right*) that established BMW's real competition heritage.

Open-topped two seater sports cars have been something of a speciality for BMW – and a great success in motorsport. The standard version of the 328 is shown *left* while the modified body style of the Mille-Miglia roadster is *below* and *below left*. The 507 (*right*) was campaigned by a young Hans Stuck at the Swiss Hill Climb Grand Prix.

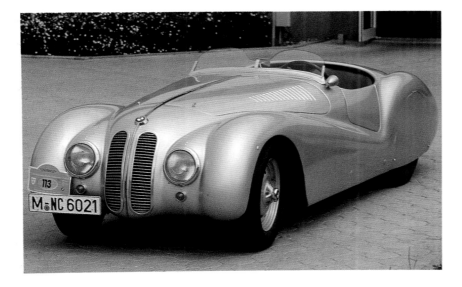

perience in car production that BMW had at the time, and the results are more than just impressive. They signal what was to come over the next 50 years.

An abbreviated version of the Mille Miglia was run in 1940 after the outbreak of war in Europe and a streamlined coupe variant of the 328 took victory with an average speed of 103.5mph – to get that high an average speed it means that von Hanstein and Baumer must have driven their 328 virtually flat out the entire course! In fact, 328s took first, third, fifth and sixth places. This was the ultimate version of the 328. With its aerodynamic all-aluminum bodywork weighing a mere 93 pounds, these 135bhp machines were capable of 125mph. Obviously with the outbreak of war, this was the end of the first session of BMW's motorsport history but at least the company finished with a flourish.

As explained elsewhere in the book, the end of hostilities meant that BMW's major Eisenach plant was now in Eastern Germany. Renamed EMW, the new company actually produced derivations of pre-war 2 liter models for competition. The first model was heavily based on the 328 and called the S1.

From 1953, EMW produced its own 1.5 liter sports racing car which was quite successful until 1956 when the company decided to cease any form of motorsport.

Back on the Western side of the wall, BMW's serious financial problems obviously meant that motorsport was the last thing on the list of necessities for the German manufacturer. Despite this, BMWs were still seen in various formats built by small specialist racing concerns (Veritas, AFM, Monopol). These and a number of one-off machines based on BMW derivations achieved a number of successes in sports car racing and Formula Two.

For the mother company, however, there was no successor to the all-conquering 328. Only the glorious V8-engined 507 that was announced in 1956 had any sporting pretensions – but as we have recalled, as a production proposition it was far from being a commercial success. Despite that, a number of 507s did find their way into international hill-climbs where the model registered a number of victories; the records show that the Swiss Hill-Climb Grand Prix was won by a BMW 507 driven by a certain Hans Stuck – a name to remember! Competition on the hills in those days was tough, this branch of motorsport being far more high profile than it is today. There were a number of Ferraris that found themselves humbled by the talent of Stuck and the 507's 150bhp V8.

As you can imagine, there were not any competition versions of BMW's Isetta bubble car. However, the 700 saloon that followed was a different story. The Type 700 RS was a special works version that looked like the road-going versions and of course used all the components, but the significant difference was that the engine, tuned to produce 70bhp at 8000rpm, was moved forward ahead of the rear axle not behind it as on the production models. Other important features were the tubeframe chassis and shortened wheelbase. This model was also one of the first that was tuned by outside racing concerns with direct support by BMW (a philosophy that has worked so well for the company over the years). One of the major independent set-ups that had success with the 700 RS was the Martini Tuning Company of Nurburgring that developed an 85bhp version capable of 118mph. While the BMW 700 RS model represented the return of BMW to the touring car ranks, where it achieved a number of significant class vic-

Left: A 2002 Turbo in full flight in a 1989 club race. For many owners this beautifully kept example would be too valuable to allow near a race track.

Right and below right: BMW's battle with the might of Ford of Germany and its impressive Capris was the highlight of sedan racing in the 1970s. In the end, the BMW 3.0CSL triumphed . . . repeatedly.

tories, it was not until the arrival of the new 1500 model in 1962 that BMW began really to climb back to the sort of competition success that it had been enjoying in the 1930s.

In 1964, a BMW 1800 Ti scored its first victory in a touring car race at Trier driven by Hubert Hahne — another name that would become synonymous with further BMW victories. In that year the BMW 1800 Ti won 27 out of 28 races. When his car was uprated to the 2000 Ti in 1966, Hahne was the first driver in any class of sedan to lap the old Nurburgring circuit in less than 10 minutes. Two years later came the 2002, with works prepared versions producing 200bhp, and the model stomped on its touring car competition from the likes of Alfa Romeo and Porsche. The 2002 enjoyed a relatively long reign at the top of the touring car tree, until the introduction of the 2 liter BDA version of the Ford Escort. To combat this, the 2002 Turbo was introduced but its success was curtailed by a change in the rules which made the model ineligible for competition. BMW, however, had an answer to that as we will relate.

In the field of single-seaters, BMW debuted a prototype 2 liter for the 1966 Aldrans hill-climb in Innsbruck, Austria. The four cylinder engine had four valves per cylinder with twin overhead camshafts and a power output of 260bhp. Mounted first on an ex-Formula One Brabham chassis, this unit was then modified to meet the new 1967 regulations for Formula Two. In 1.6 liter form it gave 225bhp and was fitted to a Lola T100 chassis and raced by John Surtees in his Lola race team. The engine proved unreliable and heavier than its competitors but BMW was not to be deterred.

In 1969 the company began its own Formula Two team. Initially BMW used a development version of the Lola chassis before new Len Terry-designed chassis were available. A new cylinder head design was introduced to the engine. Two cars, and sometimes even three, were fielded in events but the results were poor and at the end of the year, disaster struck the team when driver Hans Mitter crashed his BMW during practice for the German Grand Prix and was fatally injured.

For 1970 BMW had Jackie Ickx and Jo Siffert on the driving staff together

with regulars Hahne and Dieter Quester. This was a much better package; Hahne won Hockenheim, Siffert won at Rouen, Ickx at Salzburg and Tulln-Langenlebarn, and Quester at Neubiberg and the final round at Hockenheim. A successful year was crowned by the surprising decision from the board at BMW to withdraw from racing altogether. This move was reversed almost as quickly as it was made and BMW Motorsport GmbH set up as a separate operation in Munich in 1972 with the aim of both establishing works team involvement and offering technical support and assistance to various other companies that wanted to run BMW chassis and engines. It was after this move that BMW tasted its first real single-seater success when the British March team used the German engines in their own Formula Two chassis. The 315bhp, 1999cc engines powered March-BMW machines to no less than six European Formula Two Championships. At the height of the success in Formula Two, no less than two-thirds of all grids ran BMW engines. Understandably this led BMW to consider the even greater step up to Formula One, but more of that later.

BMW in motorsport really means sedan cars and the race circuits of the 1970s reverberated to the unique sound, stunning speed and outrageous bodywork of the multi-winged BMW CSLs. For many, this writer included, this was the golden age and BMW was the golden team.

Ford in Germany were the masters of the larger-engined class in the European Touring Car Championship at the turn of 1970 with the highly successful 3 liter versions of Ford of Europe's Capri, built and raced from Cologne. They were, therefore, arch rivals to BMW and so it was all the more remarkable when Ford's competition manager Jochen Neerpasch defected from the Cologne team to set up the new BMW Motorsport department in Munich. Neerpasch and his assistant Martin Braungart had been responsible for the all-conquering Ford Capri program so the move was little short of sensational at the time. Their achievements at BMW were impressive. With Braungart in charge of chassis preparations and Paul Rosche head engineer working on the 3.3 liter straight six engine, the famous BMW Batmobile was born.

Racing BMW M1s were an awesome sight. The Procar series was called by some cynics a pure publicity stunt by the German company. Whatever the case, the spectacle of these mid-engined monsters roaring around race tracks pleased all who loved motorsport.

The new BMW CSL was ready to race on 1 January 1973 but early testing had shown a number of engine problems and a tendency for the car to over-steer dramatically – this tail-wagging characteristic was never more pro-nounced than when the car was being driven by Neerpasch's own racing pro-tégé, Hans Stuck. The car was assigned to a wind tunnel and reappeared sporting outrageous aerodynamic appendages, hence the nickname Batmo-bile. First reaction in racing circles was to scoff at these rather ridiculous-looking coupes, until Hans Stuck slashed an amazing 15 seconds off the lap record at the old Nurburgring circuit.

The era of the 'lightweight BMWs' as they were known, was a long one (in racing terms). Interestingly, the BMWs were actually heavier than their main competitors the Ford Capris even although they had been lightened by making the doors, hood and trunk lid in aluminum with the side and rear win-dows plastic. Six versions of the BMW CSL won the European Touring Car Championship between 1973 and 1979. BMW was supporting a number of private teams, notably Alpina and Schnitzer, which helped when the factory actually reduced its own works program. It seemed to make sense to let others take the glory, after all it was still a BMW first past the flag regardless of who had prepared the car.

The drivers during this period remain household names today. For in-stance, when Dieter Quester and Toine Hezemans won the 1974 Champion-ship they beat a similar Alpina car driven by James Hunt and Jackie Ickx. Chris Amon and Hans Stuck were also in the works team while the top men in the Ford camp included Jackie Stewart and Jochen Mass. Niki Lauda and Jody Scheckter also drove in the championship as did the then reigning World Champion in Formula One, Emerson Fittipaldi. Unfortunately you don't get that kind of top quality in this form of racing today but it does at least help to underline the importance of the BMW domination during this period.

Motorsport regulations change almost as frequently as the British weather and it would take up far too much space here to try and explain what happened throughout this period and how it effected BMW. All you really need to remember is that the BMW CSLs were essentially road cars, heavily modified for racing. In 1976 Europe's sporting authorities introduced Group 5 regulations which were collectively known as the silhouette formula; a racing car's overall shape had to look like a road car, but underneath it could be a pure racer. The shape, however, did not include the wheel arches (which could be extended to cover larger wheels and tires) or any additional spoilers and wings. For this new format, BMW built the 320i. The rules stated that only the engine block had to be original and so the 1990cc four cylinder for-mat of the road car was used but tuned to produce an impressive 300bhp. This was used by the BMW Junior Team – a set of young drivers entered by the factory for the German Championship. These included Eddie Cheever, Marc Surer and Manfred Winkelhock. It was obviously good training as all three of these drivers eventually made it into Formula One.

As we have previously explained, the BMW Motorsport department has also been responsible for the M Sport road cars. This exciting range began with the M1, a two seater sports car that had a complex and protracted birth. The car was very much the baby of motorsport chief Neerpasch who wanted to develop from scratch a car to continue the company's racing successes. To meet the regulations of the time and homologate the M1 into European Group 4 regulations, a total of 400 models had to be built in a year. It is hardly surprising, given all the problems, that this did not happen the first year. However, instead of missing out on racing this exciting new machine, BMW worked with the Formula One Constructor's Association to organise the Procar series.

Procar was a superb piece of promotion for the car and for BMW in parti-cular. The Procar races ran after the last practice sessions at a Grand Prix

(but before the actual race) with the five fastest GP drivers stepping into five specially prepared M1s. The rest of the field was then completed with privately entered BMW M1s.

The Procar series came in for its fair share of criticism during its two seasons. Nevertheless it was a great promotion and produced some spectacular racing. The M1 also competed in regular racing but with limited success. In turbocharged format, the 3.2 liter engine was claimed to produce nearly 1000bhp but in events like the Le Mans 24 Hours the car was outclassed by the likes of Porsche. It could all have been so different if the car had been built and homologated into racing closer to its 1975 announcement date. During the four years that passed before it made it to the start line, a great deal changed in racing. Bearing that in mind, the Procar series was something of an inspiration.

A number of BMW M1s did make it to North America to race in various sports car championships but BMW's real success has always been in Europe. BMWs have dominated the European Touring Car Championship winning no less than 16 times in the period from 1966-88. BMW made an even more significant mark in Formula One when it matched its single seater knowledge with the wealth of information its engineers had been collecting on turbocharging race engines and entered the Grand Prix circus with a brand new power unit.

Engines of eight and twelve cylinders had been the familiar sight along the Grand Prix pit lanes until Renault surprised everyone with a turbocharged 1.5 liter V6 unit. Not instantly successful perhaps, but it did show what could be possible. BMW introduced a far less mechanically complex unit based on the four cylinder block that had first seen the light of day in the 1960s. Indeed, its very age was what had attracted BMW's head engineer Paul Rosche, 'well-seasoned' blocks being preferred to brand new designs.

The unit had many similarities with the successful Formula Two engine; the cylinder head was virtually identical. However, fitted with its KKK turbocharger, the unit produced some 570bhp right from the start of testing. The unit's relatively small size meant that Brabham's designer at the time, Gordon Murray, was able to produce a very clean and distinctive chassis for the new power unit. The car started testing in mid-1981 and actually raced for the first time in South Africa in January 1982. It immediately proved to be exceptionally quick and was the fastest Formula One machine in a straight line, topping the speed trap at 198mph. As time went on great progress was made and considerably more power was found from the unit, especially during qualifying practice when 1000bhp was often rumored. Rather less than that was needed during the races and back at Kyalami in the fall of 1983 for the South African GP, Nelson Piquet took his Brabham-BMW BT 52 to third place and clinched the Formula One World Championship. It was the first time that the Championship had been won by a turbo power unit.

Left: BMW power units have been used in a number of different formulae. This is a URD in the Group C World Endurance Championship.

Right: The BMW M3 has been all dominant in its class of sedan racing in various national championships. This is Ian Forrest in the 1989 British Touring Car Championship.

Below: A striking yellow M535i in race trim.

M3s at play! Scenes from a variety of British sedan car races. The talented James Weaver (*above left*) narrowly missed winning the 1989 British Touring Car Championship in his M3 by a single point. As you can see from these pictures, M3s come in all sorts of color schemes, some catch your eye and some you just want to walk away from.

Even more M3s. . .

Below left: Frank Sytner has raced BMWs for a number of years. It is a good way for him to advertise his business as Frank sells the cars and his is the only company outside Germany licensed to build Alpina BMWs.

Overleaf: In motor racing, it often comes down to team work. This is the impressive Schnitzer team readying its cars for battle.

1983 was, however, the highpoint of the BMW Formula One program and it was wound down in 1987. A new era, again a reflection of BMW's ability to meet any new motorsporting regulations, was to begin. And it would be with BMW doing what it does best – racing sedans. But don't get the idea that BMW's racing roots had been forgotten while it made its mark in the glamorous world of Formula One. Far from it. With the changing regulations in motorsport introducing Group A rules (this means that some 5000 production versions have to be built for a model to be homologated) a BMW 528i in the hands of Helmut Kelleners and Umberto Grano took the 1982 European Touring Car Championship. A year later, for the fourth time in 14 years, BMW stalwart Dieter Quester took the title at the wheel of a 635CSi. This particular car was built and raced by the now very successful private Schnitzer team. This was probably the most successful private outfit at the time and in 1986 Roberto Ravaglia clinched both the European title and the prestigious 24 Hours of Spa at the wheel of this rapid coupe.

FISA, the international motorsport authority, announced in 1987 that there would be a World Touring Car Championship. And BMW had exactly the right car for that, the new M3. Not an outright winner, with its normally aspirated engine it cannot match the power of the turbocharged Sierra Cosworths, but it has proved unbeatable in the 2 liter class. The 300bhp M3 took the European Touring Car Championship as well as no less than seven National titles in its first year. Roberto Ravaglia was crowned World Touring Car Champion in 1988. The M3 has proved to be the most successful racing BMW in its first season. It also grabbed the company's first ever World Rally Championship victory when Bernard Beguin brought an M3 home first in the 1987 Tour de Corse. That M3 was prepared by David Richards' Prodrive team which is based in Silverstone in Britain.

Rallying has not, a little surprisingly perhaps, been something that Munich has wanted actively to support. It seems that BMW would like to keep its M3s away from nasty muddy forests. It is known that BMW was not too interested in David Richards' initial proposal that he wanted to rally the new

M3. Interestingly, this has not always been the case. In 1969, the factory debuted the 2002Ti in the Monte Carlo Rally. Neither of the cars entered finished the event but the factory continued to dabble with rallying until 1974. A seeming victory in the 1972 Portuguese TAP Rally was the closest you can get to an event that we would recognise in present day World Championship terms. The driver then was Achim Warmbold (now running Mazda's 4wd rally effort) and co-driver Jean Todt (the man behind the very successful Peugeot Talbot Sport) and the pairing also took the prestigious Alpine Rally – an event you will remember BMW first won back in 1929. Unfortunately the pair were disqualified from first place in Portugal and Munich's enthusiasm for this particular branch of motorsport has never been the same since.

It could have been so different. In 1973, Martin Braungart left his BMW Batmobile racers in Munich and brought a rather special 2002 to Britain for Bjorn Waldegaard to use in the RAC Rally. The car only weighed some 1000kg and yet produced about 220bhp from its Schnitzer built 2 liter engine. Remember that this was during the period that the Ford Escort was the all-conquering rally car and Waldegaard's persistence in chasing Timo Makinen's leading Escort is all the more impressive. Granted he threw the little BMW into the trees on one stage and had to be satisfied with only seventh place, but it certainly proved that it had the potential, properly developed, to give the Escort a run for its money.

As this is being written, therefore, the immediate motorsporting future for BMW rests with the M3 and increasing touring car racing success on the circuits of Europe. What the future holds is as much in the hands of those who make the rules for international motorsport as it is with an individual manufacturer like BMW. However, there is much pressure on the Munich manufacturer now that rivals Mercedes-Benz have returned to racing and claimed the top spot in World Sports Car racing, gaining victory at the 1989 Le Mans 24 Hour Race. It also seems possible that Porsche may return to Formula One with a new engine. Bearing that in mind, BMW's next move will be interesting but the company is well up to the challenge.

Tomorrow's BMWs

The future is now. At least it is with BMW. Any progressive manufacturer must invest in the future, and that means investing in its own research and development departments. BMW, however, is doing rather more than that. BMW has a brand new research and development department that is actually involved in building cars for sale. Enter the Z1.

In 1986, BMW began to build a unique specialised research and development complex just north of its Munich headquarters. This Research and Development Center, known within the company as FIZ, has cost a staggering $600 million and covers an area of well over 1 million sq ft. The complex incorporates design, workshop and production areas. When fully operational with research, suspension and drivetrain engineering departments, some 6500 people will work there. FIZ is responsible for the coming generations of BMW cars with the key fact being that all the necessary departments are housed under one roof. This is a facility that few manufacturers have.

Obviously investment of this magnitude must be expected to offer long term, rather than immediate, gain. However, in the case of BMW there is already a direct result with the latest two-seater sports car, the Z1.

The striking Z1 was first shown at numerous Motor Shows where the company cleverly judged public reaction, but did not officially confirm that there were plans actually to build the model. To all but the most knowledgeable BMW historians it undoubtedly seemed a little incongruous for a company known for its sporting sedans to want to build such a machine. But when you look into it more closely, the Z1 is a natural successor to the 328 and the 507, two superb examples of open-topped motoring, one a sales success, the other a notable failure.

The Z1 was the brainchild of the newly formed BMW Technik GmbH research and development company and as such it has a number of innovative design ideas. The great thing about the Z1, however, is that it did not remain just a good-looking prototype and in January 1989, it went into full production. That was only three years since its initial conception and as far as new car gestation periods go, that's a lightning quick birth — especially when one considers the number of revolutionary ideas that are included.

It would be quite easy just to think of the Z1 as a front-engined, rear-wheel-drive two-seater sports car that uses the already proven 325i mechanicals. Easy, but totally wrong. To start with it has a composite-fiber sandwich floor-

pan. This is exceptionally light – only 33 pounds – can carry high loads, is obviously corrosion resistant and permits the Z1 to have a very smooth and, therefore, aerodynamic underside. In addition BMW engineers calculate that it adds 10 percent to the monocoque's torsional stiffness. Obviously if you have an open-topped design, it needs to be very rigid to prevent it flexing. The Catch 22 situation, of course, it that it is difficult to do this without having a roof, or at least an unsightly roll-over bar. With the Z1, the monocoque chassis is galvanised and has a zinc filling between the welds. This increases

rigidity by a claimed 25 percent, add that to the composite floorpan, deep side sills, the rear cross panel and the strong tube that is integrated within and connecting the windshield pillars and you have a light but exceptionally rigid chassis structure. There is a complete absence of scuttle shake, the perennial problem with open-topped machines the world over. But the engineers did not stop there. Innovation continues on the Z1 with its injection-cast thermoplastic body parts. All non load-bearing body panels are removable for ease of repair, with the possibility that BMW will make body

Previous page and this page: The new BMW Z1 is undoubtedly the most stunning BMW yet built. It is also the most technically interesting. The car has been built by the independent Reasearch and Development Company, BMW Technik. With its steel monocoque chassis, plastic bodyshell and vertically retracting doors it sets new standards for sports car design.

Oh look, no doors! The doors on the BMW Z1 slide down into the sill for ease of access and open-topped, open-sided motoring.

Below: Just plug in and drive away. BMW is seriously looking at other forms of propulsion for its car range. The electric car is still a way off commercially but with battery technology improving, who knows?

panels available in different colors so that owners can change the look of their Z1 when the mood takes them. A final novelty for the chassis is in the rear silencer which is transversely located under the tail but is actually 'wing-shaped' to work as an airfoil and cut down lift.

Such significant automotive design developments are not obvious to the untrained eye, but that is not what you can say about the Z1's doors – or rather its lack of them. The Z1 does not have conventional opening doors, preferring to have the side panels slide down to thigh level at the touch of a button. With the 'doors' down and the roof off, the Z1 offers true open top motoring. To enjoy this to the full, you need a sports car to have a well-engineered soft top and the Z1 has exactly that. Following from the company's experience with the convertible 3 Series, the Z1's soft top folds down and completely out of sight under a neat rear panel. With the top up there is a distinct absence of wind noise that makes the Z1 a true all-the-year-round sports car.

With such a light monocoque, the Z1 was always going to be a winner in the power-to-weight ratio stakes. Fitting the 2.5 liter fuel-injected 170bhp version of the six cylinder gives crisp performance with 60mph occurring in just under eight seconds and a top speed of 136mph. This car can be a high speed cruiser for the speed restriction-free sections of the German Autobahn as well as a spirited runner in search of the winding country lanes or glorious hairpins of a mountain climb. However, it is the Z1's performance that has been the model's only criticism. The car is so good, it could handle much

more power. When this book was being researched, that question was raised and one top executive within the M Sport department in Munich did admit that there were those who would like the Z1 to be included under their roof. The plan, even if it is only at the level of bar room banter, would be to fit the Z1 with the M3 engine, thus giving it 215bhp. BMW, as a company, has recently proved that it is not slow to seize an opportunity, so who knows?

The impressive handling characteristics of the Z1 are also owed to the innovative nature of the R&D team. It would obviously have been easy to slot the rear suspension trailing arm set-up from other BMWs into the back of the new sports car. Instead, there's a completely new 'Z-axle' which will in fact be seen in future 3 Series models. The Z1 has a 49/51 weight distribution, thanks to the positioning of the engine behind the front axle line and that, added to the newly developed double wishbone and Z-shaped longitudinal links, gives road holding and handling that is in the supercar league. It really is that good.

The motoring world was impressed when it saw the design study version of the Z1, 'but they'll never build it,' muttered the cynics. They were silenced in the best possible way when the model was officially produced as BMW Technik's first car. As this was being written in the summer of 1989, production was up to six cars a day and total production was going to be, according to BMW, left to demand. The demand is likely to be there for some time if the initial black market for UK models is anything to go by; the first few Z1s in Britain were reportedly changing hands for £50,000-£60,000 ($80,000) and that was more than double the official list price in Germany.

The other recent model to be heavily influenced by the work of the R&D department is the new 8 Series range (see Chapter Two). This is the range of cars that is going to lead BMW into the 1990s and so it was vital that they were seen to be significantly improved, even if only to justify the high retail price. Indeed, the Munich R&D department actually built the first few 8 Series models with the 24 valve Motorsport version of the 3.5 liter six cylinder as fitted to the M5. That unit offers 315bhp, which despite being an impressive figure, will pale into insignificance when the four-valve per cylinder 5.4 liter V12 8 Series is launched, for which a power output of around 400bhp is likely.

Interestingly it is the rear of the new 8 Series on which the R&D engineers have had most influence because like the Z1, the 8 Series models have a completely new rear axle and suspension set up. BMW has developed its trailing arm suspension as far as it will go, and while it has engineered out some of the disadvantages, particularly the nasty tail-happy characteristics that plagued early models, the engineers looked for something completely new for the 8 Series. The resulting rear end has no less than five separate links on each side of the suspension to provide anti-dive and anti-squat control, camber control and to cut out the effects of load reversal due to hard cornering or rapid lane changes. This is perhaps the most impressive quality of the new suspension. Despite the copious amount of power available, the car is not designed to be a handful to drive and, in the event of needing to do a lane change or swerve at high speed, the 8 Series BMW will handle it all without drama. High speed sporting sedan yes, but highly safe as well.

The 8 Series also has a development of the electronic damper control (EDC) that BMW has developed with Boge and already fitted to the 7 Series and the M3. The system works by having each shock absorber fitted with an electro-magnetic valving control which can offer soft, medium or hard settings. The system can switch between different settings in less than 40 milliseconds. The electronic brain receives inputs about what is happening from sensors at the right hand front and rear wheels, taking account also of vehicle speed and steering angle. What that means is that, according to the way the car accelerates or reacts to bumps in the road, the dampers on each corner of the car will stiffen or soften to ensure that ride comfort is maintained and matched with stiffer settings when cornering hard.

The new car will be packed with electronics, as well as the 'usual' engine management systems. Anti-lock braking, anti-slip control and a tire monitoring system are also fitted. With this, the driver will be alerted to any loss in pressure, he can then call up a display of each tire's pressure which gives the recommended maximum speed under those particular load conditions.

With all this electronic wizardry it's not surprising, perhaps, to find out that BMW is researching the production potential of an all-electric car. With growing public awareness of the environmental problems related to exhaust emissions, the 'clean' electric car has always been thought to be the answer. The trouble is that battery technology is not up to it; lead acid batteries can-

From the outside it just looks like a BMW, but underneath. . . This electric car development program has progressed far. It was started back in 1972 and a number of engine options have been tried. The latest one (*left*) is the closest that BMW has come to a full production possibility. Interestingly, because the weight and size of the batteries meant that they had to be placed low down in the rear of the car, this has turned out to be BMW's first front wheel drive vehicle!

not store enough power to give the sort of performance that people would now demand. There have, however, been some significant developments with the sodium-sulphur battery and that is what is used in an innocuous looking BMW 3 Series. The car is capable of a top speed of over 60mph and has a range of 90 miles. Over the next couple of years BMW engineers are confident that they will have further raised that to over 75mph and a 125 mile range. The car's DC electric motor delivers 23bhp continuously and can provide 50 foot-pounds of torque. Interestingly because the batteries had to be positioned lengthways at the rear, BMW had to use the shell of a 325i four-wheel drive model, BMW's first electric car is, therefore, also the company's first front-wheel drive. The car is close to being a feasible manufacturing proposition as a city car and the drawback is not so much in speed or range but due to the fact that at present the batteries are very expensive and do not last very long, six months at most. When that situation changes, as it doubtless will, BMW could have one of the first electric production vehicles.

Overleaf: The architecture of BMW's corporate headquarters is deliberately designed to be reminiscent of the company's famous badge.

All photos this page: A hydrogen powered car is close to being a production possibility from BMW. Hydrogen is a popular alternative to fossil fuel but it has to be kept at a very low temperature and this makes the insulation of the fuel tanks both difficult and expensive. BMW's next move is to try and get a supercharged version of the V12 engine running on hydrogen and producing comparable horsepower. When that happens, it might find its way into the showroom. Tomorrow may not be that far away.

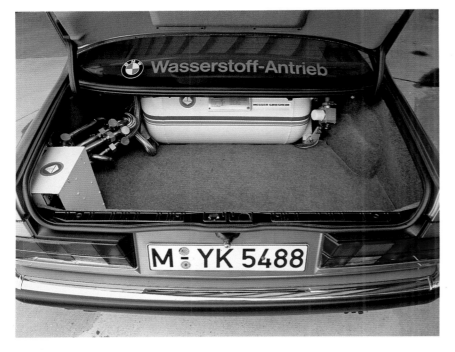

It's unlikely, however, that electric cars will completely replace internal combustion vehicles in the near future but BMW is conscious that the decline in fossil fuel reserves will mean an alternative source of energy will be needed. The favorite alternative at present is hydrogen. This has many advantages since you can convert a 'conventional' piston engine to run on it, and it is also almost pollution free. The problem is that you need rather a lot of it and so storage is a problem. The best method of storage is in liquid form

which means that the hydrogen must be kept at a temperature of minus 235 degrees Centigrade. Therefore, very careful insulation of the tank is necessary and that is the expensive bit.

BMW's first hydrogen powered car appeared 10 years ago and at present the engineers are working on a model based on the 735iL. They have found that direct injection (similar in principle to the process used in the diesel engine) of the hydrogen produces the best results. With the aid of a supercharger the converted 735i has around about 134bhp, compared to 204bhp for the unsupercharged conventional model. That is still not really enough, which has led the R&D department to look at the V12 engine and the aim is to have a twin-supercharged V12 giving the same 300bhp as the standard version. BMW is convinced that the hydrogen car will come, but that it is not ready for acceptance yet.

BMW is also a member of Prometheus. Sounding like the star of a science fiction B-movie, Prometheus is a group of 12 car producers across Europe and stands for Program of a European Transport system with Highest Efficiency and Unprecedented Safety. Quite a mouthful, but highly laudable as the aims relate to vehicle safety. One of the successes so far has been the development of vision enhancement systems using infra-red cameras for driving at night or in fog. This technology is available today but there are a great many legal problems in allowing a driver to look away from the road at any form of TV monitor.

The FIZ department is also looking at new materials, the use of ceramics for engines, active noise suppression and traffic guidance systems. And these are just the projects that the company is prepared to talk about. What else is happening behind the closed doors of the new research facility we can only guess. But, if the result is as good as the Z1 one can hardly wait for those doors to open.

Index

Page numbers in *italics* refer to illustrations

ABS brake system, 42
acceleration,
    3.0, 32
    3.0CSi, 34
    323i, 38
    750i, 48
    Alpina, 78
    Batmobile, 34
    M1, 62
    M3, 66
    M5, 65
    M535i, 69
    M635CSi, 70
    Z1, 105
aerodynamics,
    CSL, 91
    M3, 66
aircraft engines, 8, 15
all-wheel drive, 45, 51
Alpina Burkard Bovensiepen AG, *75-7*, 76, 78, *79-81*, 81, 91
Alpine Trials, 9, 10, 84
Ambi-Budd, 20
Ammerschlager, Thomas, 66
Amon, Chris, 91
Austin Seven, 9
axles,
    8 series, 105
    850i, 54
    Z1, 105

badges, *8, 9*, 45, *62*, 65
Batmobile, 34, *34-5*, 88, 91
batteries, 105, 107
Baur, 28, 38, 46, 62
Bayerische Flugzeugwerke, 8
Beguin, Bernard, 97
BFW Helios, 8
BMW Bayerische Motoren Werke,
    and Alpina, 76, 78
    finance, 16, 28, 46, 87
    formation, 8
    and Mercedes-Benz, 8-9, 15
    and motorsport, 10, 31, 66, 70, 81, 84-97
    research and development, 46, 102
    and World War II, 15, 26
BMW cars,
    2.5CS, 32
    3.0CS/3.0CSL, 32, 34, *34-5*
    3/20 PS, *9, 10*, 10
    3 series, 16, *38-9*, 38, *44-5*, 44
    3 series Touring, *50-1*
    303, 10, *20*, 20
    315, 10, *84-5*
    315/1, 84
    319, 10, *84-5*
    319/1, 84
    320i, 91
    325i Convertible, *44-5*, 46
    325i Touring, 51
    325iX, *45*, 45
    326, 10, *12-13*, 15
    328, 10, 15, *19, 22*, 22, *23, 84-5*, 84, 87
    328 Mille Miglia Roadster, *22, 86-7*
    335, *14*, 15
    5 series, 16, *36-7*, 36, *43*, 43, *52-3*, 52
    501, 15, 26
    502 V8, *26*, 26
    503, 15, *16*, 26, *27*
    507, 15-16, *16, 28-9*, 28, *87*, 87
    510, *26*
    525e, 43
    528i, 97
    535i, *93*
    6 series, 16, 41
    635CSi, *40-1*, 97
    7 series, 16, *42*, 42, 46, *47*
    700, 16, *28-9*, 28
    735i, 78
    750i, *48-9*, 48
    8 series, 105
    850i, *8, 54-6*, 54
    1500, 16, *30*, 31, 76
    1602, 31
    1800 Ti, 88
    2002, *30*, 31, 88, 97
    2002 Turbo, 16, *32-3*, 32, *88*
    2002Ti, 31, 97
    2002Tii, 16, 31
    2500, 32
    2800, 32, *33*
    2800CS, 32
    Alpinas, *75-7*, 76, 78, *79-81*, 81, 91
    Batmobile *and see* CSL, 34, *34-5*, 88, 91
    Cecotto M3, 67
    CSL series, 34, *34-5*, 88, *89*, 91
    Dixi, *9*, 9-10, *10*, 20, *21*, 84
    Frazer Nash cars, 10, *11, 14, 19, 22*, 22, 84
    Isetta, 16, *17*, 28, 87
    M1, *59-61, 90-1*, 91-2
    M3, *58-9, 65-6*, 67, *83, 93-7*, 97
    M5, *43*, 43, *62*
    M525i, 36
    M535i, *67*, 69, *70*
    M635CSi, 41, 70, *71-3*
    M Sport, 16, 36, 43, 58-81, *68-9*, 91
    Mille Miglia Roadster, *22, 86-7*
    Roberto Ravaglia M3, 67
    Targa, 31
    Touring, 31, 51
    Type 55 Frazer Nash, 10
    Type 700 RS, 87-8
    Z1, *102-4*, 102-3, 105
BMW motorcycles, 16
    Helios, 8
    R32, *8, 9*
BMW Motorsport GmbH, 46, 52, 58, 62, 88
BMW Technik GmbH, 102, 105
BMW-Steyr Motoren GmbH, 16
bodywork, 20, 22, 62, 87, 91
Bovensiepen, Burkard, 76
Brabham-BMW, 78, 92
brakes,
    5 series, 52
    501/502, 26
    7 series, 42
    Dixi, 20
    M3, 66
    M5, 65
Braungart, Martin, 88, 97
bubble car *see* Isetta

cabriolets, 20, 28, 38, 46
Castiglioni, Camillo, 8
catalytic converters, 48, 78
Cecotto, Johnny, 67
Cecotto M3, 67

chassis,
    3/20 PS, 10
    Lola, 88
    Z1, 102-3, 105
Cheever, Eddie, 91
convertibles *see* cabriolets

Dixi, *9*, 9-10, *10*, 20, *21*, 84
doors, Z1, 105

Eisenach Car Factory, 9, 20
electric cars, *104-7*, 105, 107
electronic damper control (EDC), 52, 105
electronics, 7 series, 46
emission laws, 78
EMW cars, 15, 87
engine management systems, 42, 52, 66
engines, 10
    3 series, 38, 44
    303, 10
    325i Touring, 51
    5 series, 36, 43, 52
    501/502, 26
    6 series, 41
    7 series, 46, 48
    700, 28
    8 series, 105
    850i, 54
    1500, 76
    2002, 31
    Alpina, *78*, 78, 81
    Dixi, 9-10, 20
    for Formula One, 78, 92
    four cylinder, 31
    M1, 62
    M3, 66
    M5, 65
    M535i, 69, *70, 73*
    M635CSi, 70
    Renault, 92
    six cylinder, 10, 20, 22, 26
    Type 700 RS, 87-8
    V12, 48, 81
    V8, 15-16, 26, 28
    Z1, 105
European Touring Car Championships, 32

Falkenhausen, Alex von, 28
Fielder, Fritz, 10
Fittipaldi, Emerson, 91
Ford, 88
    Capri, 91
    Model T, 9
Formula One, 76, 78, 83, 92, 97
Formula Two, 88
four-wheel drive, 45, 51
Frazer Nash, 10, *11, 14, 19, 22*, 22, 84
Friz, Max, 8
fuel injection, 31, 32, 36, 42

German Touring Car Championship, 78
Giugiaro, Giorgio, 58
Goertz, Count Albrecht, 16, 26, 28
Grands Prix *and see* Formula One, 84
Grano, Umberto, 97
Gustav Otto Flugmaschinenfabrik, 8

Hahne, Hubert, 88
Helios motorcycles, 8
Henne, Ernst, 84
Hezemans, Toine, 91

hill-climbing, 87, 88
Hoffman, Max, 16
homologation specials, 66
Hunt, James, 91
hydrogen powered cars, 109

Ickx, Jackie, 88, 91
instrument panels, *44*
Isetta, 16, *17*, 28, 87
ItalDesign, 58

Karmann, 41
Kelleners, Helmut, 97

Lamborghini, 58
Lauda, Niki, 91
Le Mans 24 Hours, 10, 84
Lola, 88

March-BMW, 88
Martini Tuning Company, 87
Mass, Jochen, 91
Mercedes-Benz, 8-9, 15, 32, 54
    190E, 69
    300SL, 26
    350SL, 34
Michelotti, 16, 28, 31
Michelotti and Denzel, 16
Mille Miglia, 10, 22, 87
Mille Miglia Roadster, *22, 86-7*
Mitter, Hans, 88
monocoque bodies, 28, 31, 62, 102-3
Monte Carlo Rally, 9, 97
Moss, Stirling, 10
motorcycles,
    BFW Helios, 8
    BMW R32, 8, *9*
Motorsport *see* BMW Motorsport GmbH
Murray, Gordon, 92

Neerpasch, Jochen, 58, 69, 88, 91
Nurburgring, 10, 84, 88

Otto, Gustav, 8
Otto, Nikolaus August, 8

Piquet, Nelson, 76, 78, 92
Popp, Franz Josef, 8-9
prices,
    Alpina B12, 81
    M1, 62
    Z1, 105
Procar races, 91-2
Prodrive, 97
Prometheus, 109

Quandt, Herbert, 16, 31
Quester, Dieter, 88, 91, 97

R32 motorcycle, 8, *9*
racing cars, 10, 31, 66, 70, 81, 84-97
racing regulations, 78, 81, 91, 97
radiator grilles, 20
rallying, 34, 97
Rapp Motorenwerke, 8
Ravaglia, Roberto, 67, 97
Richards, David, 97
Roberto Ravaglia M3, 67
Rosche, Paul, 88, 92

112 **INDEX**

sales of cars,
   328, 10, 22
   503, 26
   507, 28
   700, 28
   Dixi, 9, 10
   M1, 62
   M3, 67
   M5, 65
Scheckter, Jody, 91
Schnitzer, 91, 97, *98*
Siffert, Jo, 88
silencers, Z1, 105
silhouette formula, 91
speeds,
   3.0, 32
   3.0CSi, 34
   315, 10
   323i, 38
   328, 22, 87

6 series, 41
503, 26
700RS, 87
750i, 48
1500, 16, 31
2002, 31
2002 Turbo, 32
2800, 32
Alpina, 78, 81
Batmobile, 34
Dixi, 9
Formula One, 92
M1, 62
M635CSi, 70
Z1, 105
steering wheels, *51*, 65, 78
Stewart, Jackie, 91
Stuck, Hans, 87, 91
Surer, Marc, 91
Surtees, John, 88

suspension,
   3 series, 44
   5 series, 36, 52
   501/502, 26
   8 series, 105
   850i, 54
   1500, 31
   Alpina, 78
   M1, 62
   M3, 66
   M5, 65
   M535i, 69-70
   M635CSi, 70
   Z1, 105
Sytner, Frank, 78
Sytner of Nottingham, 78, *97*
Todt, Jean, 97
transmission,
   503, 26
   7 series, 46

Treaty of Versailles, 8
turbochargers, 78

Waldegaard, Bjorn, 97
Warmbold, Achim, 97
Weaver, James, *94*
wheels,
   2002, 31
   Alpina, 78
   M3, 66
   M5, 65
Winkelhock, Manfred, 91
World Touring Car Championship, 97

Acknowledgments

Special thanks to BMW(West Germany) and BMW(GB), Royal Ascot Garage, Miss Betty Haig, Nick Calviou and Dick Lovett Ltd, Swindon.

BMW: pages 4-5, 6-7, 8(both), 9(both), 10(both), 14(below), 15(both), 16(below), 20, 21, 23(below), 26, 27(below), 29(top), 30(top), 33(below), 35, 36, 38, 39, 45(top), 48(below), 54(both), 55(both), 56-57, 58, 59(top), 62, 63(both), 74-75, 79(both), 80(both), 81(both), 82-83, 84(top), 86(top), 87(both), 98-99, 100-101, 104-105, 106(both), 107(all 3), 108(both), 109(both), 110.
Neill Bruce: pages 11, 12(both), 13(both), 14(top), 17, 18-19, 22(both), 23(top), 24-25, 44(both), 45(below), 46, 47(below), 49(both), 52(both), 53(below), 60(top), 61(both), 84(below), 85(both), 86(below).

Norman Hodson: pages 59(below), 64(below), 67(top).
Andrew Morland: pages 28, 29(below).
Don Morley: pages 90(both), 91, 92(top).
National Motor Museum, Beaulieu: pages 1, 16(top), 27(top), 30(below), 31, 34(both), 41, 43(top), 48(top), 50(both), 51(both), 53(top), 60(below), 65, 66(top), 67(below), 68, 69(all 3), 70, 76, 77, 78.
Maurice Seldon: page 93(below).
Colin Taylor Productions: pages 32, 33(top), 88.
The Research House: pages 37, 42(both), 71, 72(both), 73, 89(both).
Stuart Windsor: pages 2-3, 40, 43(below), 47(top), 64(top), 66(below), 93(top), 94(both), 95(both), 96(both), 97, 102(both), 103(both), 104(top).
Design by David Eldred.
Picture Research by Maria Costantino.